THE STRAIGHT LEAD

THE CORE OF BRUCE LEE'S
JUN FAN JEET KUNE DO ®

THE STRAIGHT LEAD

THE CORE OF BRUCE LEE'S JUN FAN JEET KUNE DO®

Teri Tom

Tuttle Publishing
Tokyo · Rutland, Vermont · Singapore

First published in 2005 by Tuttle Publishing, an imprint of Periplus Editions (HK) Ltd., with editorial offices at 364 Innovation Drive, North Clarendon VT 05759.

Library of Congress Cataloging-in-Publication Data
Tom, Teri.
  The straight lead : the core of Bruce Lee's Jun Fan Jeet Kune Do /
Teri Tom.—1st ed.
    p. cm.
  Includes bibliographical references.
  ISBN 0-8048-3630-2 (pbk.)
  1. Jeet Kune Do. I. Title.
  GV1114.6.T66 2005
  796.815—dc22
                        2005028717
Distributed by

North America, Latin America & Europe
Tuttle Publishing
364 Innovation Drive
North Clarendon, VT 05759-9436
Tel: (802) 773-8930
Fax: (802) 773-6993
info@tuttlepublishing.com
www.tuttlepublishing.com

Asia Pacific
Berkeley Books Pte. Ltd.
130 Joo Seng Road
#06-01/03 Olivine Building
Singapore 368357
Tel: (65) 6280-1330
Fax: (65) 6280-6290
inquiries@periplus.com.sg
www.periplus.com

Japan
Tuttle Publishing
Yaekari Building, 3rd Floor
5-4-12 Ōsaki
Shinagawa-ku
Tokyo 141 0032
Tel: (03) 5437-0171
Fax: (03) 5437-0755
tuttle-sales@gol.com

First edition
08 07 06 05   10 9 8 7 6 5 4 3 2 1

Printed in the United States of America
Designed by Stephanie Doyle
TUTTLE PUBLISHING® is a registered trademark of Tuttle Publishing.

To Mom, who showed me how to write my first paragraphs

And

Dad, who taught me there are no shortcuts.

And for Sifu Ted—thank you for all that I've learned through JKD.

C O N T E N T S

Special thanks to:

Shannon Lee Keasler and Concord Moon LP

Paul G. Hewitt

Lance Lobo and the Laureate Press

Ray Knecht for the photo shoot at the Sports Club/LA. You truly are
"the finest sports and fitness club company in the world."

Richard Bustillo for allowing us to shoot photos at the IMB Academy

Denis Trantham at Westside Studio

And I am forever indebted to my "A" team:

Winnie Cheng, our photographer extraordinaire,
who saved the day with her camera and thoughtful eye.

John MacClean, a fine JKD instructor in his own right,
for posing for our instructional photos.

Bradford Akerman, my Mac guru.

Janice Parente, research expert and *consigliere*.
As with everything you touch, you have elevated the quality of this book.

Ted Wong, thank you for your time, your patience, and your good,
good heart. No one has been more loyal to Bruce Lee. It is because of
your integrity and persistence that his legacy will be preserved.

Wesley and Janice Tom. You've supported me through thick and thin
(a lot of thin!) and provided me with enough opportunities for several lifetimes.
Thank you. None of this would have been possible without your love.

F O R E W O R D

by *Shannon Lee Keasler*

I first heard about Teri Tom's book when Ted Wong gave me a call and told me he had a student who had written a very good book on the *Jeet Kune Do* (JKD) straight lead and was interested in incorporating some pictures of my dad, quotations, and the like, into her manuscript. Ted had nothing but good things to say about Teri, and instinctively I knew that the book must be worthwhile.

Ted Wong has been a family friend and student of JKD since before I was born. He is my *sifu*, and when it comes to the preservation and truth of my father's art, there is no one better—no one more dedicated, knowledgeable, or thoughtful. He is not driven by fame or fortune or accolades. He is simply an unfettered soul with a pure heart, a clear mind, and a steady body. If he says something is good, I know I can trust that.

After our first conversation about the book, Ted presented me with some sample chapters and information about Teri. After reading her sample pages (and ultimately the entire manuscript), I was impressed. Teri's ability to deliver the information clearly and concisely was instantly gratifying. The depth of her research is remarkable and her insight into the subject matter sound. I knew right away that her grasp was solid and that she was, of course, a student of Ted's. Reading her words has done my heart a lot of good. I am grateful for her writing ability. The text is fluid and well structured. It is a pleasure to read. Teri's research acts as a solid base upon which her instruction in JKD can stand firmly and securely. Her scientific explanations are pure and perfectly Jun Fan Jeet Kune Do. I am delighted.

Over the years, a lot of damage has been done to Bruce Lee's art of Jeet Kune Do. Many people have done the art a disservice because they do not truly understand it. JKD is a scientific, physical, and philosophical art of individual combative expression that is, above all things, simple and direct. That bears repeating: *simple and direct.* JKD is not an amalgamation of many different arts. It is not mixed martial arts. It is not an accumulation of weapons, but rather a paring down and a focusing. To become sentient in your martial ways—to spring out of the void and return to the void with ferocity and collectedness—takes years of honing your skills, not the accumulation of an overloaded arsenal. Further, JKD is not a philosophy devoid of technique. One cannot divorce the science from the philosophy or divorce the techniques from the principles. There has been a lot of egregious misrepresentation and too much misinterpretation. And so, a book such as Teri's that is designed to shed a true light on many important aspects of JKD, in particular the straight lead, fills me with hope and inspiration. This is a book that makes an effort to present its material fully and decisively, and succeeds in doing so. For this I am grateful.

In the months to come, Bruce Lee's immediate family will be working to fully launch its nonprofit Bruce Lee Foundation for the preservation and proliferation of Bruce Lee's legacy, philosophy, and art. This art we now call (as does Teri on the cover of her book) Jun Fan Jeet Kune Do, as a way to more specifically delineate it as the authentic art of Bruce Lee as he taught it in his lifetime.[1] In the near future, anyone seeking instruction will be able to find solid information and referrals on our Web site (www.bruceleefoundation.com). The Foundation will be doing a lot more in the years to come to further our aim of preservation. But right now, if you want to learn something about Bruce Lee's art, you can read Bruce Lee's own writings (available in several different publications) and you can *read this book.*

My thanks to Teri and to Ted for their hard work and their dedication to my father and his art.

In the spirit of Jun Fan Jeet Kune Do ~

—Shannon Lee Keasler, April 2005

Notes

[1] The trademark of Jun Fan Jeet Kune Do® has only recently been recovered by the Bruce Lee Foundation after a lengthy legal battle. Its reclamation is one of the first steps in reversing over thirty years of damage to Bruce Lee's art. For more information about the name, please see the final section of this book, entitled "Parting Shots."

F O R E W O R D

by *Ted Wong*

Didn't see it coming! That wasn't an unusual thought for me when sparring with Bruce Lee. This punch was elemental, powerful, and fast—very fast. It was the straight lead, a punch absolutely basic to Lee's contemporary martial art, Jeet Kune Do—or as he referred to it, *scientific street fighting.*

JKD's discipline is one of specifics, the foundation of which Bruce Lee developed not only by deconstructing Eastern martial arts, but also by exploring the history of Western boxing and fencing. He scoured hundreds of books on the science of combat, the laws of physics, and the styles of Western fighting. The depth and intensity of his study can be witnessed in the copious notes, the underlined passages, and the wear and tear of the books that were his special sources of inspiration. In discovering the straight lead, Lee found a punch to serve as a keystone to his fighting form. And he found the straight lead's impressive effectiveness described, most notably, in the writings of boxers Jack Dempsey and Jim Driscoll, and fencer Aldo Nadi.

The art of fencing held a particular resonance for Lee. The straight lead's extension of the arm in a swift, direct movement operated as a line of attack comparable to fencing's straight thrust—*Western sword fencing, without the sword,* was how Lee described it. Both moves convey the essential principle of his fighting form—the principle of interception. Jeet Kune Do, meaning "The Way of the Intercepting Fist," is a perfected synthesis of Western fighting elements—and a discipline that has impacted all of martial arts.

Lee once asked me what was the most important thing in a fight. When, after a dozen tries, I still hadn't found the answer, he told me it was adaptability—the ability to adjust, to find your feet when confronted with changing situations. He explained that the traditional martial arts, at which he was adept, had become lost in their traditions—traditions that proved too elaborate, too awkward, too slow when executed in real fighting situations. Lee adapted. He spent years experimenting. When he found an approach he liked, he submitted it to an empirical test—he'd find out if a punch or kick worked by doing it. If it didn't operate properly, he would try again until *all of it* was right—the intent, the mechanics, and the speed at which it all comes together. The defining and refining of JKD evolved over time through Lee's rigorous examination and physical effort. It represents Bruce Lee's lasting legacy. To honor this legacy, JKD must be taught and learnt the *right way*—not any old way.

Figure 1: *Ted Wong on the receiving end of a straight lead thrown by the master himself.* (© Linda Lee Cadwell)

An inspiring teacher, Lee never forced students to learn more than they could handle. He taught in stages, encouraging each student to understand and absorb at his or her own pace. By accepting only a small number of students, Lee sought to gradually impart his art, an art that was new and revolutionary for its time—one that could easily be misinterpreted or sloppily executed if not cultivated in the proper way. As a student and friend of Bruce Lee, and as a teacher of JKD for some thirty-five years, I continue to admire the realism, effectiveness, and physical and intellectual beauty of his fighting system.

Lee was an extremely precise person. In everything he did he paid attention, almost obsessively, to detail. There's no question that he saw the big picture in relation to JKD—what it represented, and what it delineated. This is evident in his writing, in his speaking, and in the way he presented himself to the world. But as with anything new and original, imitators and pretenders to the throne are rife. Without Bruce Lee here to combat them, the integrity of JKD has been undermined over time.

I choose not to forget what is genuine and true to Bruce Lee's legacy—what I was taught. What has been needed, for years, is a clear-cut approach that can rectify and correct the muddled interpretation and unnecessary additions to JKD. A step in that direction is offered here by Teri Tom who, with exacting care, lays out the straight lead—where the punch came from, how it operates, and how it's connected to the heart and soul of JKD. She backs up her instruction with extensive research that parallels Lee's own.

Teri Tom approached me almost seven years ago for lessons in JKD. A slight young woman with no prior knowledge of martial arts, Teri posed a challenge. But I believed that with proper instruction, the principles of Lee's system could work for her. At each step of the learning process, Teri surprised me again and again, with her committed resolve and perceptive application of the discipline. She has been a dedicated student, logging in over one thousand hours of instruction, as well as many more hours of sparring. And in those hours of sparring, she has developed a picture-perfect straight lead. Truthfully, I have not seen anyone else—with the exception of Bruce Lee, that is—throw a lead punch that is as fundamentally sound and technically refined. She's a natural straight shooter with both the front and rear hand. She also happens to pack a mean right hook. What she may lack in physical strength and size, she makes up in technical know-how.

Teri's physical prowess is matched by an intellectual strength. Showing a sincere curiosity about the origins of JKD, she read and absorbed the published works of Bruce Lee and the authors who inspired him. When she proposed a book on the straight lead punch, I encouraged her to take up the task. I gave her access to my own archive of Bruce Lee materials, which includes photocopies of many rare books and notes from Lee's own library—all highlighted and annotated by Lee himself. Using this material has allowed Teri to see how he came to the conclusions he did regarding Western boxing and fencing, and what aspects he chose to integrate into his unique fighting system.

In retracing Lee's footsteps, Teri is thoughtful and clear in her words. Altogether, she presents a truly accurate perspective on the development of the straight lead, and a truly meaningful contribution to the study and appreciation of Jeet Kune Do and the man who created it, Bruce Lee.

—*Ted Wong, October 2004*

INTRODUCTION

"THE CORE OF JEET KUNE DO"

I t may seem a bit excessive to devote an entire book to a single punch, but as Bruce Lee himself declared, "The straight punch is the core of Jeet Kune Do."[1] To write a book on the Jeet Kune Do straight lead, then, is to write a book on the most basic, fundamental principles of JKD. In fact, the entire structure of the art was designed around the most efficient and forceful delivery of the straight punch. Strategically, you must have a strong lead hand for both offense and defense. Other weapons—hook punches, rear crosses, uppercuts, and kicks—are of little use without a good lead hand to set them up.

The culmination of years of scientific study, the straight lead is a biomechanical marvel maximizing the potential for leverage, accuracy, acceleration, and force production. Once you have grasped the mechanical principles behind the straight lead, you will be able to learn other JKD punches and kicks with greater ease.

NO MYSTIQUE

By Bruce Lee's own admission, though, the straight lead is the most difficult technique in the Jeet Kune Do arsenal, and of the art itself, he said, "Only one of 10,000 can handle it. It is martial art. Complete offensive attacks. It is silly to think almost anyone can learn it."[2] And as Ted Wong has said of straight punching, "If it were easy, everyone would be doing it."[3]

However, the exclusivity of JKD has nothing to do with exotic, ancient hoodoo voodoo. There are no mysterious secrets steeped in mythology or rigid classicism. No, these are the very things Bruce rebelled against. If anything, Jeet Kune Do laid everything about the martial arts out in the open. Instead of being shrouded in mystery, its principles are rooted in the sciences of biomechanics, physics, and fencing strategy.

The scientific principles behind JKD are not difficult to grasp, nor is the physical conditioning required to practice it particularly difficult to achieve. What makes Jeet Kune Do and the straight lead so challenging is the patience needed to take a few simple techniques and stay with them—the perseverance to refine, refine, refine, knowing that you will never achieve true perfection. Even so, the problem is not necessarily that people lack discipline. In many cases, they just haven't been given the scientific information to convince them to stick it out.

In writing this book, then, I am stating the case for simplicity and refinement. Everything presented here starts with Bruce Lee, and where possible, I have referenced his published work. Because of Bruce's untimely death, however, he never left us with a comprehensive guide to the straight lead, so wherever I could, I have traced Bruce's writings to their original sources in the works of Aldo Nadi, Jack Dempsey, Jim Driscoll, Edwin Haislet, Roger Crosnier, and Julio Martinez Castello. All other material appearing in this volume is what I have learned directly from Ted Wong.[4]

The purpose of this somewhat academic approach is to demonstrate that Jeet Kune Do is not a mere smorgasbord of styles. It is true that Bruce was heavily influenced by Western boxing and fencing, and, yes, he incorporated some grappling techniques into his system. But he did not haphazardly throw styles together, as some would like to believe. No, Jeet

Kune Do is its own system, with its own set of carefully researched and honed techniques. As you will see throughout this book, those things Bruce chose to incorporate evolved from a history of fighting science that dates back thousands of years.

You will also notice that Bruce did not choose *everything*. He went with the thumbs-up-power-line punch over the more modern boxing jab, the rebellious cocked left heel over the orthodox grounded heel, the rapier over the broadsword. There were reasons behind these choices. It is the aim of this volume to reveal those reasons.

THE ROOTS OF JKD

No technical Jeet Kune Do book would be complete without first looking at what Bruce called the roots of JKD. They are:

1. Physical ingredients
   - On-guard positioning
   - Footwork and movement
   - Postures in relaying force

2. Underlying ingredients
   - Balance
   - Economy of form
   - Intuitive expression of self in applying force and releasing speed
   - Organic quiet awareness—continuity of being
   - Totality in structure and consciousness of the whole
   - Efficient mechanics
   - Capability to regulate one's rhythm as with the opponent's, plus the ability to disturb same
   - Strong, dominating aura to flow with or against the "harmonious unit"
   - Having no public
   - Sincerity and honesty
   - To function from the root[5]

The on-guard stance, footwork, relaying force, balance, economy of form, efficient mechanics. Remember the roots, for they are the foundation of all JKD techniques—not just the straight lead—and they are the guiding principles of this book. When we speak of simplicity and refinement, we are talking about the roots. When you are lost, confused, or unsure of your technique, go back to them. They are your roadmap.

A Few Words of Encouragement

Straight hitting is no simple task. Bruce said so, as did all his major boxing influences—Edwin Haislet, Jim Driscoll, and Jack Dempsey. "The ability to hit straight from the shoulder is not a natural act," wrote Haislet. "It cannot be learned by chance and experience does not teach it. Straight hitting, with body behind each blow, is an art that takes years of study and practice to perfect."[6] *Years.* You do not learn the straight lead overnight. Beginners often try it for a few weeks, become discouraged by their lack of power, and give up, reverting to their old ways. They later wonder why their progress plateaus, but as the saying goes, the definition of insanity is repeating the same action, over and over, expecting different results. Learning the straight lead may require you to step out of your comfort zone for a little while.

Yes, swinging punches look spectacular. Yes, that modern boxing jab feels more natural. But as you'll soon see, there's a difference between natural and scientifically effective. With this volume, I hope to present enough scientific evidence and strategic arguments to convince you to stick with the straight lead. Weigh the evidence yourself. As you progress through the various stages of learning—from awkward baby steps of neuromuscular programming to the advanced stages of combative application—I ask that you take a small leap of faith. Trust in the instruction presented here. Stay with it. The secrets that are hidden now will someday reveal themselves to you.

Finally, given that we live in a fast-paced world of instant gratification, it's easy to see why straight punching, which takes years to cultivate, has become something of a lost art. It's nice to know, however, that there are still some things that money cannot buy. The straight lead is one of them. There is just no substitute for time invested in any endeavor—for patience, hard work, experience, sweat, and, in this case, probably a little blood! So while other arts may focus on the accumulation of endless techniques, may stress the flashy over the efficient, or even allow the buying of belts, remember that you are on a different path. Stay on it. Use the roots as your roadmap, and the rewards will pay off big, in ways you cannot imagine.

At times you may be discouraged, as others on the quick and easy road seem to pass you by. You may be tempted to follow the crowd. To this, I offer the following from Jack Dempsey:

> Let me emphasize again that you will feel very awkward when you first try the moves in long-range punching. I stress that awkwardness for two reasons: (1) so that you won't figure you're a hopeless palooka, and (2) so that you'll pay no attention to wisecracks of friends or sideline experts who watch your early flounderings. Remember: He laughs last who hits hardest.[7]

In the seventeenth-century martial arts classic *The Unfettered Mind*—a book, by the way, that resides in Bruce Lee's personal library—Takuan Soho had a similar message:

> If you follow the present day world, you will turn your back on the Way; if you would not turn your back on the Way, do not follow the world.[8]

So with these words in mind, let's begin our exploration of the Jeet Kune Do straight lead.

NOTES

[1] Bruce Lee, ed. John Little, *Jeet Kune Do: Bruce Lee's Commentaries on the Martial Way* (Boston: Tuttle Publishing, 1997), p. 21.

[2] Ibid., p. 59.

[3] In conversation with Ted Wong, June 8, 2004.

[4] See the Ted Wong interview in this book for his Jeet Kune Do credentials.

[5] Lee, ed. John Little, *Jeet Kune Do: Bruce Lee's Commentaries on the Martial Way*, pp. 385–386.

[6] Edwin L. Haislet, *Boxing* (New York: A.S. Barnes & Noble Company, 1940), p. 7.

[7] Jack Dempsey, *Championship Fighting: Explosive Punching and Aggressive Defence* (New York: Prentice Hall, Inc., 1950), p. 25.

[8] Takuan Soho, trans. William Scott Wilson (New York: Kodansha International Ltd., 2002), p. 14.

A BRIEF HISTORY OF STRAIGHT PUNCHING

E verything comes from something, and the straight lead is no exception. In 1964, Bruce Lee wrote, "The art of straight hitting (punching in a straight and direct line) is the foundation of scientific skill. It is the end result of thousands of years of careful analysis and thought."[1] Indeed, the straight punch is not something that "just happens." Its origins can be traced to the pre-Olympic era (1500 to 1000 B.C.).

Judging from artwork and pictures, it is believed that blows were originally delivered by swinging and hooking. This is a primitive fighting method and is actually observed in bears and cats—hence, Jim Driscoll's reference to swinging, uneducated fighters as "Bear-Cats."[2] Images from Minoan and Greek vases, friezes, and statues from the pre-Olympic era provide evidence that the Greeks were starting to utilize the left, or lead, hand. The position of the lead hand in these pictures suggests the development of straight punching.

The *caestus*, the original boxing glove, provides further evidence of straight punching. The caestus was really nothing more than a leather hand wrap, which covered almost the same areas that its modern-day cotton descendant does. In particular, the caestus provided protection over all four fingers, between the second joint and knuckle, the hitting surface of straight punches.[3]

Hand protection for straight hitters was later reinforced during the Olympic period with the introduction of the "hard glove," a thick leather glove that, again, covered the four fingers between the second joint and knuckle, the surface of all straight hitting. Even though fighters of this era were still swinging, the hard glove's hitting surface is evidence that those swings were now shortening into more scientific hooks.

Along with the prominence of straight hitting came the boxing stance that very much resembles the modern boxing stance. In Greek artwork depicting boxing scenes, the left (lead) foot is clearly in front of the right foot, with the left hand held straight out. Even then, the left hand was used as a defensive tool to fend off opponents with pestering jabs, from a stance that guarded the centerline. The Greeks probably used the lead hand as a gauge for judging distance as well.[4]

Whatever progress the Greeks had made, however, was soon lost when the Romans introduced the lead-loaded caestus, which was quite effective at smashing skulls, ending matches swiftly and spectacularly, regardless of the contestants' skill. Following in the vein of the loaded caestus was the *myrmex*, a pick attached to the caestus, intended to pierce body parts—nasty, nasty business. Both weapons may be blamed for the loss of fistic art and science. In a situation not unlike the one we face today, the desire for bloody entertainment had brought fighting to its lowest common denominator.

It would take 1200 years and the development of fencing for boxing to reemerge. As John V. Grombach wrote in *The Saga of the Fist*:

> When boxing did come back in England, it was introduced by fencing-masters. As a result, the boxing stance was made to approximate the fencing stance and to good effect. By that time, fencing had advanced to the point where the small sword or thrusting weapon was preferred to the broadsword or sabre. The use of the straight thrust or lunge against any side sweep or slash had been developed. The principles of advancing, retreating, much of our modern boxing footwork, and our straight punching came from fencing.[5]

The rapier was the weapon that established the supremacy of straight thrusting over slashing.[6] First, the rapier, with its pinpoint accuracy, was much more effective than the broadsword in finding those vulnerable little areas between plates of armor. But the main advantage of the rapier over the broadsword is that the shortest distance between two points is a straight line. Applied to fencing or boxing, a straight thrust or straight lead will reach its target before a swing, hook, or sweeping slash. Straight motions in fighting are, therefore, not only offensive maneuvers, but defensive in nature as well.

This is what we call the "stop-hit" in fencing. As Nadi noted, "The great advantage of the stop-thrust over the counterattack-proper is that it can be performed against fast, correctly executed attacks—stopping them in their tracks."[7] The stop-hit, executed mainly with the straight lead, is such an important principle of Jeet Kune Do that this is where Bruce Lee's art derives its very name. In Cantonese, *jeet* means "intercepting" or "stopping," *kune* means "fist," and *do* is "the way." Translated in English, Jeet Kune Do is quite literally "The Way of the Intercepting Fist."

N O T E S

[1] Bruce Lee, ed. John Little, *The Tao of Gung Fu* (Boston: Tuttle Publishing, 1997), p. 59.

[2] Jim Driscoll, *The Straight Left and How To Cultivate It* (London: Athletic Publications, LTD.), pp. 16–19.

[3] Harry Carpenter, *Boxing: An Illustrated History* (New York: Crescent Books, 1982) pp. 8–10.

[4] John V. Grombach, *The Saga of the Fist* (New Your: A.S. Barnes and Company, 1977), pp. 191–194.

[5] Ibid., p. 200.

[6] Richard Cohen, *By the Sword: A History of Gladiators, Musketeers, Samurai, Swashbucklers, and Olympic Champions* (New York: Random House, 2002), pp. 28–29.

[7] Aldo Nadi, *On Fencing*, (Bangor, ME: Laureate Press, 1994), p. 185.

EVOLUTION OF JEET KUNE DO'S STRAIGHT LEAD

B
y now, the story of how Bruce Lee came to develop Jeet Kune Do is the stuff of legend, but it bears repeating here. In 1964, Bruce was teaching martial arts at his Oakland school. Other Bay Area kung fu instructors, displeased with Bruce's willingness to take on non-Chinese students, dispatched Wong J. Man from Hong Kong to Oakland with an ultimatum: close the school or throw down.

The challenge, of course, was met right there on the spot, and the two faced off, but a fight that Bruce felt should have been over much sooner lasted an excruciating three minutes.[1] Bruce hadn't trained to deal with someone who ran. After the fight, he came to the conclusion that if he'd known some Western boxing, he would have dispensed with his opponent much sooner.[2]

While it's true that Bruce originally studied and taught the classical Chinese art of *Wing Chun*, it is not to be confused with Jeet Kune Do. In a letter to William Cheung, dated January 4, 1969, Bruce admitted to having virtually abandoned Wing Chun:

> William, I've lost faith in the Chinese classical arts—though I still call mine Chinese—because basically all styles are products of land swimming, even the Wing Chun school. So my line of training is more toward efficient street fighting with everything goes, wearing head gear, gloves, chest guard, shin-knee guards, etc. For the past five years now I've been training the hardest and for a purpose, not just dissipated hit-miss training.

I've named my style Jeet Kune Do—reason for my not sticking to Wing Chun [is] because I sincerely feel that this style has more to offer regarding efficiency."[3]

By this time, Bruce had already immersed himself in the study of Western boxing and fencing. In a letter to James Lee dated July 31, 1965, Bruce wrote, "I'm having a Gung Fu system drawn up—this system is a combination of chiefly Wing Chun, fencing and boxing."[4] By 1969, he had for the most part dropped Wing Chun and the classical Chinese arts. Soon afterward, he would begin writing what would eventually be published as *The Tao of Jeet Kune Do* and *Bruce Lee's Commentaries on the Martial Way*.

Because of Bruce's untimely death, neither volume appears in a form he would have intended to publish, but from these notes, we can see the heavy influence of boxing and fencing. Entire passages are quoted from boxing sources, mainly from Jack Dempsey and Edwin Haislet, and the major arguments for using the straight lead can be found in the writings of Jim Driscoll.[5]

People have assumed that Bruce Lee turned to fencing because his brother was a fencing champion in Hong Kong, but this was probably not the case. According to Ted Wong, "People always say Bruce Lee looked into fencing because his brother's a fencer. I doubt it. There had to have been some kind of writing that connected boxing to fencing. Driscoll mentioned that connection, as did Haislet. I doubt that the main interest in fencing came because of his brother."[6] As you'll see throughout this book, Bruce made direct references to Driscoll and Haislet that clearly explain how straight punching evolved out of fencing. In fact, it seems that at one time it was common knowledge that the British had revived boxing because of fencing.[7]

The most frequently cited fencing sources in *The Tao of Jeet Kune Do* come from Roger Crosnier, Julio Martinez Castello, and Hugo and James Castello. But the crucial stance and mechanical nuances come from Aldo Nadi and appear in *Bruce Lee's Commentaries on the Martial Way*. The three major influences on the straight lead specifically are Jim Driscoll, Jack Dempsey, and Aldo Nadi.

ANGRY YOUNG MEN

If his disillusionment with the status quo is what drove Bruce Lee to develop Jeet Kune Do, it was pugilistic regression that prompted Driscoll and Dempsey to write. Both authored books in an attempt to preserve the dying art of straight punching. And though Nadi's book was fueled by his intense love of fencing, that feeling was matched by his utter disgust with the fencing practices of his time.

Figure 2: *Jim Driscoll.*

Early 1900s Welsh featherweight champion Jim Driscoll authored a series of boxing books, in an attempt to rectify the pathetic state of British boxing. Chief among these slim but highly illuminating volumes is *The Straight Left and How To Cultivate It*—a book that would eventually find its way into Bruce Lee's hands.

Driscoll lamented the decline of British boxing, which he blamed on "circumstantial evidence" that supported the effectiveness of swinging punches. Remember that primal swinging motions are observed in bears and cats. Driscoll referred to uneducated fighters as "Bear-Cats." In an unfortunate set of circumstances, a succession of Bear-Cats outweighed and overpowered a series of British boxers.

In particular, Driscoll cited the rise of the wildly swinging Frank Craig, aka The Coffee Cooler, as the reason for the "Decline and Fall of British Boxing." Because swings are easier to see and appear to have more power behind them, British spectators believed them to be more effective. Driscoll argued that had The Cooler met an educated fighter, he would not have fared well, and also dryly pointed out that just because The Cooler chewed gum while fighting, aspiring fighters adopted gum chewing to improve their fighting abilities.

Flying in the face of thousands of years of fighting science, Bear-Cats such as The Cooler led the public to the weak conclusion that swinging like an animal was more effective than straight hitting. In very little time, British fistic science backslid considerably. Driscoll knew he need look no further than the development of the rapier to argue the merits of straight punching.[8]

It is most likely that this is where Bruce Lee got many of his ideas for applying the fencing straight thrust to Jeet Kune Do. "It's Western sword fencing—without the sword," he used to say.[9] The source of that principle was Jim Driscoll, who wrote:

> And this is where the straight left comes in. Not, as is usually supposed, mainly as a mode of attack, but rather as a more effective and valuable means of keeping an opponent at a respectful distance. I have remarked elsewhere that the science of modern boxing as instituted by Figg and Broughton was, and has always remained, a material development of the art of fencing. It is practically sword fencing without the sword, and follows in all its movements, or, rather, should follow, the same principles.[10]

Compare to *The Tao of Jeet Kune Do*:

> Like a fencer's sword that is always in line, the leading jab is a constant threat to your opponent. Basically, it is Western sword fencing without a sword and the primary target is your opponent's eyes.[11]

During Driscoll's time, American boxing had not yet declined in the way British boxing had, and Driscoll cited straight shooters such as Jack Dempsey as model fighters for their straight hitting, weight transfer, and footwork.[12]

THE MANASSA MAULER

It wouldn't take long, however, for American boxing to succumb to the evils of commercialization. In 1950, Jack Dempsey published *Championship Fighting: Explosive Punching and Aggressive Defence* in an attempt to correct a situation that, ironically, he had inadvertently helped create with his hard-hitting style. Dempsey explained how his popularity resulted in a lowest common denominator approach to pugilism:

> Unfortunately, my big gates did more to commercialize fighting than anything else in pugilistic history. As a commercial enterprise, the fight-game began attracting people who knew little or nothing about self-defence. Hoping to make quick money, they flocked into boxing from other fields. They came as promoters, managers, trainers, and even instructors. Too often they were able to crowd out old timers because they had money to invest, because they were better businessmen, or merely because they were glib-talking hustlers. They mistaught boys in gymnasiums. Those mistaught youths became would-be fighters for a while; and when they hung up their gloves, they too became instructors.
>
> At this writing lack of worthwhile talent in the heavyweight division is particularly appalling. It's almost unbelievable that the heavy division should have declined so far since the days when I was fighting my way up in 1917, 1918, and 1919.[13]

All of this made Dempsey, well, fighting mad. Of *Championship Fighting*, Dempsey told biographer Roger Kahn, "I wrote it because there is such ignorance about boxing. . . . Most of the boxing I see today is just embarrassing."[14] Among Dempsey's technical complaints regarding straight hitting were the following:

- Beginners are not grounded in the four principal methods of putting the body-weight in fast motion: (a) falling step, (b) leg spring, (c) shoulder whirl, (d) upward surge.

- The extremely important power line in punching seems to have been forgotten.

- The wholesale failure of instructors and trainers to appreciate the close co-operation necessary between the *power line* and *weight motion* results generally in *impure punching*—weak hitting.

Figure 3: Jack Dempsey.

- Explosive straight punching has become almost a lost art, because instructors place so much *emphasis on shoulder whirl* that beginners are taught wrongfully to punch straight *without stepping* whenever possible.

- Failure to teach the *falling step* ("trigger step") for straight punching has resulted in the *left jab* being used generally as a light, auxiliary weapon for making openings and "setting up," instead of as a stunning blow.

- Necessity for the *three-knuckle landing* is never pointed out.[15]

Dempsey was a major influence on the JKD straight lead. Indeed, in his own copy of *Championship Fighting*, Bruce had underlined key words from the above passage. Among them were "putting body weight in fast motion," "power line," "shoulder whirl," "trigger step," and "three-knuckle landing." These are issues that we'll soon address in greater detail.

THE BAD BOY OF FENCING

Of the Straight Lead Triumvirate, I've saved the most colorful character for last: Aldo Nadi, fencing legend and four-time Olympic medalist at the 1920 Antwerp Olympics, whose off-the-strip escapades were every bit as thrilling as his fencing triumphs.

Loaded with an arrogance that is justified when accompanied by genius, Nadi's contempt for the rest of the world was also driven by an intense passion for fencing. These polarized sides of Nadi impart a sense of urgency to his treatise *On Fencing*. Among the benefits to be derived from the foil, he lists general health, intellectual acuity, body composition, scholastic achievement, values, and character building. Simply put, "Man is how he behaves sword in hand."[16]

And while Nadi was obviously driven to write *On Fencing* by his love for the sport, he too was alarmed by what he saw as the decline of his sport, particularly in America. "In matters of tradition and principle," he wrote, "I fear the word compromise cannot be found in my vocabulary, let alone in my academy."[17]

Like Dempsey, Nadi was frustrated by the dearth of quality teachers of his art:

What confounds the qualified teacher is that anyone, here, can proclaim himself a Fencing Master overnight, and get away with it. Many old masters must be turning in their graves; and if they could only join us for a while, they would certainly say something on the subject. The history of fencing tells us that this art was developed throughout the centuries via death and blood, and gradually mastered as a science by hundreds of scholars who devoted their entire lives to its study and research.

It appears that many American teachers take half a dozen lessons (perhaps from another self-appointed teacher), read hurriedly a treatise of most doubtful value, and quickly obtain a position at a suitable university, college, or high school. In a similar way, I might apply for a chair of higher mathematics, or surgery, in one of our universities. Instead of landing the job however, I might be politely escorted to an asylum.[18]

Figure 4: Aldo Nadi (Photo by Rudolf courtesy of Laureate Press).

Known for his playboy antics and apparent bitterness, Nadi developed a reputation as something of a bad boy, and this naturally spilled over into his approach to fencing technique. His raised left heel, a Nadi trademark adopted by Bruce Lee, is to this day considered bad form. "All fencing teachers will tell you to keep both feet constantly flat on the strip," he wrote. "I say—No."[19] Trying to understand this rule boggles the mind, because it is nearly impossible to maintain springy mobility while trying to keep your left heel on the ground. Try it sometime. It's almost physiologically impossible to be fast and mobile while keeping both feet flat. There's a reason why we call slowpokes flatfooted.[20]

In line with Nadi's break from tradition, it's not surprising that Bruce Lee—with his disdain for classical, rigid training lacking scientific investigation—would be influenced by Nadi's *On Fencing*. I suppose the reasons that modern fencers still practice with the heel down—even while they claim Nadi's footwork was his greatest strength—are the same reasons that modern martial artists fail to investigate the advantages of the straight lead. But what those reasons are remains a mystery.

NOTES

[1] M. Uyehara, *Bruce Lee: The Incomparable Fighter* (Santa Clarity, CA: Ohara Publications, Inc., 1988), p. 15.

[2] In conversation with Ted Wong, March 18, 2004.

[3] Bruce Lee, ed. John Little, *Letters of the Dragon: Correspondence, 1958–1973* (Boston: Tuttle Publishing, 1998), pp. 110–111.

[4] Ibid., p. 60.

[5] Ted Wong with John Little, "Bruce Lee's Lead Punch: Ted Wong Explains Jun Fan Jeet Kune Do's Most Explosive Technique!" *Bruce Lee: The Offical Publication & Voice of the Jun Fan Jeet Kune Do Nucleus*, June 2000, p. 67.

[6] In conversation with Ted Wong, June 8, 2004.

[7] Captain John Godfrey ed. W.C. Heinz, "The Useful Science of Defence" in *The Fireside Book of Boxing* (New York: Simon and Schuster, 1961), pp. 158–162. "The Useful Science of Defence" was the first printed work on boxing. Godfrey was a regular at Figg's Amphitheater. An avid fencer and boxer, he was quick to point out the natural evolution of boxing out of fencing. Published in 1747, the book was a huge commercial success, and two copies currently reside in the British Museum.

[8] Jim Driscoll, *The Straight Left and How To Cultivate It* (London: Athletic Publications, LTD.), p. 20. Driscoll summed up the evolution of the rapier:

To put my argument in other words, the "Bear-Cat" brigade are bludgeon fighters, who disdain the use of the rapier, for the simple reason that they are utterly ignorant of the finer points of the game. Yet the whole history of single combat refutes their argument. Man did not abandon the club as a weapon because he preferred the rapier as a parlour pastime, but because the sword proved itself to be the more useful weapon. And it was by similar process of discovery that the axe, which had superseded the club, gave way to the sword and buckler, then to the case of swords, until even the broadsword and sabre were abandoned in favour of the rapier.

[9] Lee, ed. John Little, *Jeet Kune Do: Bruce Lee's Commentaries on the Martial Way* (Boston: Tuttle Publishing, 1997), p. 210.

[10] Driscoll, *The Straight Left and How To Cultivate It*, p. 27.

[11] Lee, *Tao of Jeet Kune Do* (Santa Clarita, CA, Ohara Publications, Inc., 1975), p. 100.

[12] Driscoll, *The Straight Left and How To Cultivate It*, p. 13.

All the real champions and first fighters today, American and French, are "straight lefters," disciples of the old British school. Jack Dempsey, Tom and Mike Gibbons, Harry Wells, Georges Carpentier, Benny Leonard, Mike O'Dowd, Pete Herman, Eugene Leonard, Jimmy Wilde, etc., are all men who hit straight, use the left hand as it should be used, are fully aware of the fact that the feet are as important as the hands in the boxing game, and are first, last, and all the time, boxers first and *fighters* afterwards. They can fight and do. They would not be champions if they didn't. But when punching they send all their weight along behind their deliveries

[13] Jack Dempsey, *Championship Fighting: Explosive Punching and Aggressive Defence* (New York: Prentice Hall, Inc., 1950), pp. 10–13.

[14] Roger Kahn, *A Flame of Pure Fire: Jack Dempsey and the Roaring '20's* (New York: Harcourt Brace, 1999), pp. 70–71.

[15] Dempsey, *Championship Fighting: Explosive Punching and Aggressive Defence*, pp. 18–19.

[16] Aldo Nadi, *On Fencing*, (Bangor, ME: Laureate Press, 1994), p. 9.

[17] Aldo Nadi ed. Lance Lobo, *The Living Sword: A Fencer's Autobiography* (Sunrise, FL: Laureate Press, 1995), p. 375.

[18] Nadi, *On Fencing*, p. 5.

[19] Ibid., p. 51.

[20] Ibid., p. 52. Nadi's explanation for the impossibility of keeping the left foot flat:

If a fencer's guard is a as compact as it should be with feet in their correct respective positions, and legs bent to the proper degree, the left heel usually cannot help rising from the floor. So much so that most people have to practice for some time before being able to keep it as near the strip as indicated. For these people, to keep it down completely would require a terrific strain on the main tendon of the left leg; or else they would have to keep their legs insufficiently bent—and no foilsman can afford that. I insist upon this fundamental difference from the teachings of others.

THE STANCE

Before we can even throw the straight lead, we must have a place from which to throw it, and in Jeet Kune Do everything begins and *ends* with the on-guard position, the JKD stance. Going back to our roots, remember that the physical ingredients are:

- On-guard positioning
- Footwork and movement
- Postures in relaying force

And always keep in mind that these physical ingredients are determined by the underlying ingredients:

- Balance
- Economy of form
- Efficient mechanics[1]

In the rush to whale away on an opponent, people may think that the small details are trivial matters, and that simply coupling approximated gross movements with brute force is enough. But precision in executing the roots of JKD is everything. As Bruce himself argued, nothing is more fundamental than good form: "Good form is the most efficient manner to accomplish the purpose of a performance with a minimum of lost motion and wasted energy. Always train in good form."[2]

Given Bruce's emphasis on form, it's surprising to see so many people fighting with such shoddily constructed stances. Eager to hit things, they gloss over the basics of the stance and later wonder why their technique falls short. Watch a good fighter, and note the differences. Efficient fighters waste nothing. Every motion is streamlined, and that makes them fast. Better fighters are more mobile and more effective at transferring weight into their punches. Chances are that the stance of a good fighter looks a lot different from those of lesser fighters.

Proper form in executing the physical components of JKD makes the underlying elements—balance, economy of form, and efficient mechanics—possible. The rewards of good form, as you'll soon see, are increased force production, leverage, mobility, speed, elusiveness, and longevity—to name a few. Everything stems from good form.

CONSTRUCTING THE STANCE

STRONG SIDE FORWARD

There's been some dispute over which hand leads, but you only have to go to the source—Bruce Lee's writings—to find that the right hand is always referenced as the lead hand, because "in this stance, you will attack mostly with the right hand and right foot just as a boxer in his left stance uses mainly his left jab, hook, etc."[3] Of course, you only need to watch Bruce's films and sparring footage to see that the right hand is the main weapon.

MIRROR, MIRROR, ON THE WALL . . .

Before we get started with constructing the stance, I recommend that you find yourself a reflective surface to practice in front of. As you are learning the basics of the stance, the mirror will give you invaluable feedback. In the beginning, you'll need it to check your alignment, because your body doesn't yet know how to achieve the proper form. With the visual feedback, though, you'll progress much faster. As you train your body, you'll be able to wean yourself away from the mirror, and you'll be able to feel when you're doing things properly.

Which brings us to the second advantage of visual feedback. As you become more technically proficient, you'll use the cues acquired from mirror training to visualize technique. You've probably heard about the way elite athletes use mental imagery to prepare for competitive events. Our greatest athletes sometimes talk of almost stepping outside themselves and seeing themselves perform. If you train in front of a mirror correctly, your mental imagery becomes that much more vivid. Mirror training, then, is not just for beginners but for fighters of any level.[4] See Figure 5.

*Figure 5: Until you have proper body feel, checking your technique
in front of a mirror is the only way to know your form is correct.*

THE FEET

As I've already mentioned, everything begins and ends with the on-guard position. The stance was designed so that the most effective punch—the straight lead—could be initiated from this position with the least motion. To construct the stance, let's start from the bottom, the feet.

In the beginning, you'll want to find a surface like a basketball or squash court that has marked lines. Or you might want to use some chalk or tape to make your own lines. It may sound like splitting hairs, but by the end of this chapter, you'll see why we're such sticklers for precision.

Stand with your feet slightly wider than shoulders' width apart. Line your right toe up along the line so that your right foot makes about a thirty-degree angle with the line. See Figure 6.

Figure 6: *The front foot should form a thirty-degree angle with the line that points toward your target.*

Now position your left foot so that the line runs directly under the arch. Raise your left heel, à la Nadi, and turn your left toe in slightly. You should feel all the weight of your left side concentrated on the ball of your left foot. See Figure 7.

Figure 7: *All of your power originates from the raised left heel.*

Be careful not to raise your left heel so high that you have no more room from which to spring into action. An excessively raised heel will also cause you to be top-heavy, placing your center of gravity in an unfavorable position. Nadi recommended that the left heel be raised approximately half an inch.[5] See Figure 8.

You'll find Nadi's influence on JKD in Bruce's notes:

> Unlike the traditional flat-footed practice, the left heel is raised and cocked, ever-ready to pull the trigger and go into action.
>
> The left heel is the spark plug, or better still, the piston of the whole fighting machine.[6]

Compare these observations with their source, Nadi's *On Fencing*:

> The left leg is not just a prop. It is the spark plug, or better still the piston of the whole fencing machine . . . raising the heel ever so little, you cock the leg ready to pull the trigger and go into action.[7]

Figure 8: *Raise the left heel just enough, but not so high that leverage is compromised.*

What both Nadi and Bruce were trying to convey is that much of the potential energy that is unleashed by a fencing lunge or straight lead, respectively, is stored in that left foot. To properly release that energy, though, the heel must be raised, giving spring to the arch of the foot and providing a push-off point in the ball of the foot.

THE LOWER BODY

Moving up, we now need to properly align the legs. Again, they will be a little wider than shoulders' width apart, knees slightly bent. We've just discussed potential energy in relation to foot position. The same applies to the legs, for it is the left leg that will exert pressure on the ball of the foot, causing the spring so necessary to the straight lead.

Because you will want to propel all your body weight forward, you do not want to waste any extra energy overcoming unnecessary inertia. This is why you want to feel all your weight, all your potential energy, concentrated on the inside, or medial sides, of your legs. If your feet are positioned correctly, you should already be feeling this. See Figure 9.

Figure 9: *Left knee correctly turned slightly inward. You should feel all of your weight on the medial sides of your legs.*

If you feel some of your weight rolling toward the outside of your foot, you will be slower to initiate the push-off. Again, we want to waste as little energy and time as possible, so not having your weight concentrated in the optimal position prior to throwing a punch is counterproductive, a bit like running uphill. This is why the left toe should be slightly turned inward. Doing this means that we'll have less inertia to overcome when trying to spring forward. See Figure 10.

Also important to the storing of potential energy is what Bruce referred to as the "small phasic bent-knee stance,"[8] The bend in the knees gives you greater flexibility and mobility, allowing you to spring into action at will. Obviously, if you start from a straight-leg position, you have nowhere left to spring from, and, therefore, no way of generating power. From a defensive perspective, bent knees allow you to give a little when receiving punches, taking some of the force out of a blow. And perhaps the most important advantage of a bent-knee stance is that it places your center of gravity in the optimal position—in other words, it enables you to achieve balance.

Figure 10: *Left knee incorrectly turned outward.*
Your weight will roll outward, slowing your punch.

BALANCE

"Center of gravity" is simply defined as the point around which an object's weight is equally distributed. Suppose you were to throw a baseball bat. You would notice the bat wobbling around the fat end, where the majority of its mass is located. The wobbling occurs about its center of gravity. If, on the other hand, you were to throw a baseball, which is a symmetrical object, it would not wobble, because its center of gravity is located at its center. The way the human body is structured determines that our center of gravity is, for lack of a better word, the tush.

Position of the center of gravity is crucial to maintaining balance, and balance is something repeatedly emphasized throughout Bruce Lee's notes. To achieve balance, imagine a line dropping straight down from any object's center of gravity. If that line falls within the base of the object, it is balanced. See Figure 11.

It also follows, then, that the wider an object's base, the more balanced, or stable, it will be. Think of a pyramid, one of the most stable structures—wide base, low center of gravity. Raising an object's center of gravity decreases the amount of force required to tip it off-balance, or to move the center of gravity outside its base of support. In Figure 12, the model has a very wide stance, a wide base of support. If we were to draw an imaginary line from his center of gravity to the floor, it would fall within the base determined by his feet. Notice that when you have a very wide stance, you feel as if no one can knock you over. You feel stable. See Figure 12.

Figure 11: When in position, your front and back feet form two points of a triangular base. An imaginary line from your center of gravity to the floor should fall within the base of the triangle. This is the definition of "balance."

Figure 12: This stance is too wide. While extremely stable because of the lower center of gravity, mobility is greatly compromised.

If your feet are less than shoulders' width apart, you narrow your base of support, decreasing stability. Your center of gravity is raised. Notice how much less stable you feel. It would take less force to knock you over. Likewise, if you close the stance too much by lining your front toe up with the left toe, instead of the arch, you also decrease the base area and lose stability. See Figure 13 and Figure 43.

Figure 13: *A stance that is too narrow does not provide enough stability because of a raised center of gravity.*

The proper JKD stance, however, is designed to keep your center of gravity within the base determined by the placement of your feet. Your lead foot, rear foot, and trunk form the triangular base. Your foot position offsets the weight of your trunk. If we were to draw a line from your trunk to the ground, that point on the ground would be the third point of the base. I'll talk later about upper-body positioning, but at this time, just know that the slight crouch keeps your center of gravity within the base of support. The weight all around your center of gravity is equally distributed. If we were to draw a line from your center of gravity to the floor, it would fall in the center of the triangle. See Figure 14.

Keep in mind that this is the general JKD stance, in which your weight is distributed about fifty-fifty between the front and rear leg. When we get into the mechanics of the straight lead, you'll actually offset that balance slightly. Also know that while widening your stance may make you more stable, you will sacrifice mobility in doing so. Again, aim for a little wider than shoulders' width. Experiment and strike a balanced trade-off between stability and mobility.

Figure 14: *The proper stance strikes a balance between mobility and stability.*

Finally, remember that "phasic bent-knee"? One of its purposes is to lower the center of gravity, contributing to a more stable stance. Keep this in mind when we get to the chapter on mechanics. One of the most common problems JKD students run into, in executing the lead punch, is that they often will straighten their legs instead of rotating their hips. This causes two problems. One, their center of gravity overtakes their front knee. Their center of gravity, therefore, falls outside the triangular base, causing imbalance. Two, straightening of the legs raises the center of gravity, further contributing to instability. Both will result in less force production and in lack of mobility. Also know that your stance may slightly widen when you are working at kicking ranges. See Figure 15.

Figure 15: *Once your center of gravity overtakes your front knee, it falls outside the base of the triangle. You'll lose not only balance but leverage and power as well.*

On the subject of balance and stability, Bruce was heavily influenced by Edwin Haislet, who argued the importance of body alignment. The greatest contributor to balance, Haislet argued, is foot position. Your feet, of course, are connected to your legs, which are connected to your trunk, which in turn is connected to your arms. So proper alignment must start with correct foot position. The arm, according to Haislet, is merely a "vehicle of body force." The fist may get all the glory, but it's really only along for the ride. Your body does all the work. And this starts with the stance. You will have to experiment to find the width of stance for optimal stability and mobility, but always remember that your center of gravity must fall within the base determined by your foot position.[9]

THE UPPER BODY: CATS AND COBRAS AND GREASED LIGHTNING

When we discuss the JKD stance at rest, think of yourself as storing potential energy; at any moment you may uncoil and lash out with tremendous power and speed. With this in mind, you'll want to hunch your back a little, which gives you more space for uncoiling at the shoulder. This serves to decrease your target area as well and puts your right shoulder in a position to protect your chin or roll away from punches. In describing this storing of energy, Bruce had this to say:

> Slight crouch—balance evenly on your right foot and the ball of your left foot, with your knees slightly bent—more on the order of a cat with his back hunched up and ready to spring (except that you are relaxed), or like a cobra coiled in a relaxed position. Like a cobra you must be able to strike so that your touch is felt before it's seen.[10]

Compare with Nadi:

> To fence well is to be greased lightning with the potential forward speed of a coiled spring. Like the cobra, a fencer must remain coiled in a relaxed position having at the same time the potentiality of leaping from absolute immobility to top speed, power and precision. The guard position is the only position from which one can attack efficiently. Like the cobra, the fencer must be able to strike (with the point of his blade) so that his touch is felt before it is seen.[11] See Figures 16 and 17.

From Figure 16, you'll see that there is a slight bend at the waist (but remember to keep your center of gravity low), and the back is slightly hunched. The point here is that you want be slightly curled up—to protect yourself by making yourself a smaller target, but also to give yourself more room from which to uncoil. You're storing more potential energy from which to unleash that lead punch.

THE POWER LINE

When we think of stances, we usually think of a static position, an at-rest position. But we've already established that the JKD stance is designed to maximize mobility and force production. We stand in the on-guard position so that when we do hit, we'll be in the most favorable position to relay force. With this in mind, we need to consider what proper alignment will look like at the point of impact, and one of the most important elements of the stance at impact is the power line.

Figure 16: *The slightly coiled JKD stance. The back is slightly hunched, and the right hand is completely relaxed.*

Figure 17: *Side view of upper-body coil.*

The power line is the reason why we punch "thumbs up," as opposed to the palm-down fist we see in modern boxing. It's also why we use the bottom three knuckles as our striking surface instead of the top two knuckles used in other martial arts.

The power line is quite simply determined by our anatomy. If you extend your arm and make a fist, you'll see that there is a straight line from your shoulder to those bottom three knuckles, *not* to the top two knuckles.

The origins of the power line may be traced to Jack Dempsey. Chapter 9 of *Championship Fighting* is heavily underlined in Bruce Lee's copy.[12] Dempsey defined the power line as a straight line that runs from your shoulder and exits at your bottom fist knuckle. Because of the way we are anatomically structured, this is the purest, most solid point of contact. To use the top knuckles disrupts the focus of the power line.[13] I don't make the rules. We're just built this way.

In accordance with Bruce Lee's advocating of kinesthetic learning, I recommend that you try the following. Stand in front of a wall in the JKD stance. Extend your arm and fist. Rest the bottom three knuckles on the wall. Take a moment to feel the solidity of contact. Try lightly tapping the wall as you go through the motion of throwing a straight. This is how you should land every time you throw a straight lead. See Figure 18.

Figure 18: *Line up against a wall to feel the solidity of the power line.*

Now do the same thing, but with the top two knuckles resting on the wall. Do you feel how you've deviated from the power line? Instead of forming a stable straight line from your shoulder to your fist, you've actually created an angle at your wrist with your fist and forearm. Feel how unstable this is. Try tapping against the wall. Can you imagine throwing all of your body weight with your wrist in such a precarious position? This is how hand and wrist injuries occur. See Figure 19. Just thinking about hitting with those two knuckles makes me queasy!

Figure 19: *Incorrect use of top two knuckles at point of impact. Using the top two knuckles necessitates a bend at the wrist, which is often the cause of injuries.*

Now compare this with the proper thumbs-up, bottom-three-knuckles fist in JKD, as demonstrated in Figure 20. You should be feeling a lot more solid.

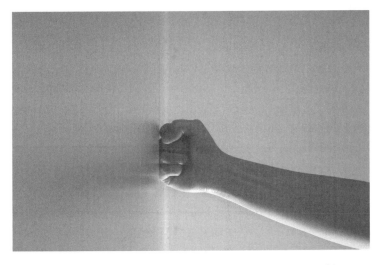

Figure 20: *Correct use of bottom three knuckles at point of impact. There is no bend at the wrist, and the power line is not disrupted.*

Keep in mind that one of the underlying principles of the straight lead design is Newton's third law, which states that when an object exerts a force on another object, that second object exerts an equal and opposite force on the first. You've probably heard it stated as, "For every action, there is an equal and opposite reaction."

Physicists will tell you that the application of force is not so much one thing acting on another as it is an *interaction* between two objects. So in our example of tapping the wall with the top two knuckles, you exert a force on the wall, and that jarring you feel through your shoulder and elbow is the wall exerting a force on you.

Another example would be the focus pads. You can only exert as much force on the mitt as your trainer is exerting back toward you. Notice that when your trainer doesn't give you much resistance, you cannot punch with very much force. But if your trainer gives you more resistance, you punch with more force (and have a lot more fun). As another example, think of trying to punch a piece of paper, versus hitting the heavy bag. No matter how hard you try, you can only hit that piece of paper so hard, because it cannot exert much force back. The heavy bag, on the other hand, allows you to hit much harder because it sends back a much greater force.

As you can see from our experiment with the power line, then, the JKD stance is designed to best withstand whatever force is coming back at you. It puts you in the best possible alignment to absorb the force returning from your punches. One of the benefits, of course, is that the power line makes for an efficient punch. Nothing is wasted. All of your force is focused and concentrated and directed toward your target. There is no dissipation at the weak links at the wrist, as is the case when a punch is incorrectly landed with the top two knuckles. In a properly constructed JKD stance, there are no weak links.

The second benefit of the bottom-three-knuckle landing is a "big picture" argument. Since the straight lead is the most frequently thrown punch in JKD, it makes sense that we want to incur the least wear and tear on our bodies from throwing it. Good form is what will keep you in JKD for the long haul. It is why Ted Wong, at sixty-five as of this writing, is still actively practicing, while many of his contemporaries have been sidelined with injuries. He'll tell you that he even hits harder than he did more than thirty years ago, and he attributes this to the sound mechanics he's honed over those years. As Bruce observed, "The older athlete regards form as a means of energy conservation and the great athlete saves energy because his extra skill makes each motion more effective—he makes fewer needless motions and his conditioned body uses less energy per movement."[14]

So if you have any intentions of practicing JKD for a long time, you must be able to feel and utilize the power line.

REAR HAND

The rear hand is positioned for protection, to parry and block blows aimed at your head. You'll want to keep your left hand close to the left side of your chin. A good left hand and judgment of distance can make you nearly impossible to hit. Parrying with the left hand also gives you a feel for your opponent's range.

You'll also want to keep your elbow close, to protect your side. By simply turning your trunk, you can deflect most blows to the body with your left arm, as shown in Figure 21.

Figure 21: *With a slight turn to the right, the left arm provides protection as you roll with the punch.*

THE FRONT HAND

To correctly position the front hand, stand in the stance as we've discussed so far, with your lead hand extended and resting at your side. Keeping your shoulder completely relaxed, bend your arm at the elbow at about a forty-five-degree angle. See Figure 22.

Figure 22: *Correct position of the front hand. There is no space between my arm and my side. This allows for complete relaxation of the arm.*

Figure 23: *Incorrect position of the front hand. The slight extension at the shoulder places unnecessary tension on the arm, which will slow your punch.*

There should be little space, if any, between your arm and your side. Holding your arm away from your body places tension on your shoulder, and you'll be wasting energy holding your arm out. This will slow you down.

Some people incorrectly think that holding your arm out gives you a speed advantage, by keeping the hand closer to the target, but it will only fatigue your poor deltoids, making you slow. As with our phasic bent knee, keeping the arm close gives you more potential energy. You have somewhere from which to lash out. If your arm is already extended, you have a tired arm with nowhere left to go. See Figure 23.

THE GUNSIGHT

Now let's be a little more precise about positioning the lead hand. Have someone stand in front of you, and with your right hand up, extend your right index finger. Where is your finger pointing? It should be toward the target, your opponent's nose. If you find yourself pointing too low—say, at your opponent's foot—readjust your hand so that you're pointing at the nose. Likewise, if you find yourself pointing at the sky, you're aiming too high. Again, adjust your hand so that you're pointing at your opponent's head. Now close your fist. This is the correct position of the hand. See Figures 24 through 26.

Figure 24: *To check if your hand position is correct, extend your index finger. It should point directly at your target—in this case, my opponent's face.*

Figure 25: Close your fist. This is your correct lead hand position.

Figure 26: From the correct hand position, shoot your fist straight out.
This is the fastest way to reach your target with the lead hand.

Think of your right hand as a gunsight. You always want to keep your target within range of this gunsight, which is your correctly placed hand. This will increase your accuracy, of course, but it will also increase your speed, because your hand is already positioned to hit the target without any other adjustments. You just shoot your hand out. No fuss, no muss.

If the hand is positioned too high or too low, you'll have to lower or raise both your hand and forearm first and then shoot out. This extra movement not only slows you down but telegraphs your attack as well. See Figures 27 through 30.

Figure 27: *If your front hand is kept too low (left),*
you'll be pointing at your opponent's kneecap.

Figure 28: *You'll have to raise your hand first, before you can fire a straight punch.*

Figure 29: *If your hand is positioned too high (left), you'll be pointing toward the sky.*

Figure 30: *Keeping your hand too high requires you to lower your hand before you can throw a punch.*

TRUNK ROTATION

I'll talk more about mechanics and hip rotation later, but let's touch on the subject here, in relation to what proper alignment looks like at impact. From the on-guard position, extend your lead arm as you rotate your hips counterclockwise. As your hip rotates, your shoulder will follow. See Figures 31 and 32.

Figure 31: *Straight lead from correct stance*

Figure 32: *Hip rotation with arm extension. Notice how this makes me less of a target by decreasing the target area. The centerline is virtually unreachable.*

Notice that as you rotate your hips and shoulders, you actually become a narrower target, making you less susceptible to counterattacks. Passages in both *The Tao of Jeet Kune Do* [15] and Edwin L. Haislet's *Boxing*[16] address this additional advantage of the stance. By the way, throwing a modern-day boxing jab does not give you this benefit. The palm-down jab does nothing to narrow your target area. It is only the straight lead that allows you to further protect the centerline as you launch an offensive.

STRAIGHT SHOOTER

We call it straight hitting for a reason. From the on-guard position, your right hand should shoot straight out and retract along exactly the same path. I've already talked about how keeping the target within range of the gunsight will keep your punch straight and improve accuracy. Another important contributor to straight hitting is the position of your lead elbow. It should be kept close to the body. If kept too far away, your target will be out of gun-sight range. Notice how you'll be pointing in the wrong direction.

Keeping your elbows close also serves a defensive purpose by giving your opponent less of a target. See Figures 33 and 34.

Figure 33: *Elbow pointing away from the body. If you were to extend your index finger from this position, you'd be pointing downward and off to the side. In order to throw a straight lead, you'd first have to center and raise the front hand.*

Figure 34: *Correct elbow position for straight lead. Keeping the elbow close to your body enables correct positioning of the hand and, consequently, more efficient punching.*

RELAX, MAX

Relaxation, both mental and physical, is something repeatedly referred to in *The Tao of Jeet Kune Do*, as it should be with all sports and martial arts. In any movement, we have something called "force-couple relationships" occurring. This means that muscles—agonists, synergists, stabilizers, neutralizers, and antagonists—are working together to create the most efficient movement around a joint.[17] To maximize efficiency, we want to minimize extraneous motion and unnecessary tension.

I've just mentioned muscles called agonists and antagonists. Agonists are prime movers that create joint motion. For instance, when we throw out a straight lead, we are performing a pushing motion. The triceps act as prime movers. Antagonists are muscles that act in direct opposition to the prime movers.[18] As we throw out a lead punch, the biceps are antagonists, because they are involved mainly in pulling motions. Therefore, they act in opposition to the triceps. As we shoot out a straight, then, we want to activate the triceps while relaxing the biceps.

As we retract the hand, though, the opposite is desirable. When we pull back the hand, the biceps become the prime movers—the agonists—and the triceps become the antagonists that we must relax.

If antagonists are fighting against the prime movers, you will be slow—and tired. It's hard enough to fight an opponent; you don't want to be fighting yourself as well. Maintaining unnecessary tension wastes energy. This is why we want to rest the right arm against our side instead of holding it away from the body. Keeping the arm away from the body requires unnecessary contraction of the muscles to hold it up. Your deltoid has to work overtime just to keep your arm in that position. Then, already in a fatigued state, it must throw out a punch. If you see a fighter constantly holding the lead arm away from the body, you already know that he or she will not be fast with the lead hand.

Likewise, being in a general state of tension—mental and physical—will also slow you down. If the agonists and antagonists are simultaneously activated, the prime mover must overcome the counteraction of the antagonists before it can perform the desired movement. Again, you will be slow, slow, slow.

Of course, this is all easier said than done. True relaxation is only achievable once you have mastered the mechanics. Proper form and mechanical sequence have been designed to maximize agonist muscle activity while minimizing antagonist activity. This is a matter of neuromuscular programming, which only comes from hours of practice. And mental relaxation can only be developed from experience in combative situations.

Failure to completely relax antagonists while trying to employ prime movers is obviously counterproductive. So, as my favorite Dinah Washington song goes, "Relax, Max."

BODY FEEL

Before concluding this chapter on the stance, and as we prepare to delve into footwork and straight lead mechanics, I'd like to stress the importance of body feel. The adoption of any new posture (stance) or movement requires a complex process of neuromuscular programming.

Think about all the new information your body must process. There's sensory information, which includes both external and internal input. External input comes from the environment, such as the kind of surface on which you're moving—grass versus concrete, for example. Internal information may come from sensory organs—for example, the muscle spindles in your muscle fibers sense the length of your muscles and the rate at which their length changes.

Sensory information must then be interpreted by your nervous system, to allow your body to respond appropriately. This is your nervous system's integrative function. The nervous system then sends the information to effectors, motor neurons in your muscles, so that your muscles will perform the correct response. Pretty amazing, isn't it?

As you learn a new technique, your body is making all sorts of new neural pathways. Your nervous system is programming your body to assimilate information and respond in a specific way.

Perhaps the stance has felt a bit awkward so far. That's all right. Your body is simply trying to program itself into maintaining that position. The reason that I stress body feel, however, is that you want to make sure you are programming correctly. It makes no sense to do things incorrectly, develop bad habits, have to break bad habits, and then reprogram.

In the *Tao*, Bruce referred to this as kinesthetic perception or *"getting the feel of it."* It's important to note that he was not just talking about movement but was referring to "postures"—the stance—as well.[19]

All physical training is kinesthetic learning. I emphasize its importance because there are many things I discuss in this book that will be imperceptible even to the trained eye. As we start putting ourselves into motion from the stance, this will become more apparent, but it all starts with the stance.

Do not just emulate what you see in these illustrations. Be sure you are feeling the sensations that I describe. Is your right shoulder completely relaxed? Do you feel all of your weight and potential energy in the medial sides of your legs? Is all the pressure concentrated on the ball of your left foot? Do you feel the solidity of the power line when landing with the bottom three knuckles? Is your left heel raised just enough or too much?

The heel is an excellent example. That critical half inch or inch too high is something your instructor might not be able to see. Everyone is a little anatomically different. You'll have to feel it out. If your heel is raised too high, your center of gravity will be raised as well, and you will lack stability. Too low, and you may lose springiness. Bruce encouraged the "[investigation] of 'body feel' to relay different parts of foot tools (heel, ball, instep) to [the] target."[20] *Always* take the extra time to stop and ask yourself how a particular alignment, posture, or technique *feels*.

Simply going through the motions is not enough. The fact that your feet and arms are aligned similarly to those in the illustrations doesn't mean that you are completely in the correct stance. You must feel all that potential energy in your left foot. You must feel your center of gravity striking the correct balance of mobility and stability. And when you hit it, when it feels good, take note of it. Remember it. Let your body remember it.

Returning to the roots of JKD: "Real knowledge breeds 'body feel.' Surface knowledge breeds mechanical conditioning."[21] Once you are familiar with the basics of the stance, listen to your body. On the way to refining your mechanics, your body will learn how to put itself in the best position to generate force and transfer it to the target. JKD is not just a cerebral endeavor. It's physical. Real understanding of the straight lead means that your body—not just your head—understands.

SEE FOR YOURSELF

We've talked a lot about body feel. Here's a little experiment you can try that will enable you to feel for yourself what makes the straight lead so effective.

First, line up in the correct JKD stance. Have a friend apply force by hitting your fist with the palm of his hand. Take a moment to note how your body absorbs that force. See Figures 35 and 36.

Figure 35: *Correct JKD stance.*

Figure 36: *Apply force to JKD stance and note feeling at impact.*

Now stand in a traditional Wing Chun stance (see Figures 37 and 38), squarely facing your opponent, fist extended as it would be at the point of contact. Notice how you feel off-balance when your partner hits your hand. Where do you feel your body taking most of the blow? The shoulder? The elbow? The hips?

Figure 37: Wing Chun stance.

Figure 38: Apply force to Wing Chun stance and note feeling at impact.

Next, move from your Wing Chun stance into a modern boxing stance (see Figures 39 and 40). Imagine a straight line pointing straight to your target. Align your right toe so that it forms a thirty-degree angle with this line. The arch of your rear, or left, foot should be directly over this line with the heel down. Have your partner hit your fist again. You should feel even less of the force.

Figure 39: Modern boxing stance with heel and palm down.

Figure 40: Apply force to boxing stance and note feeling on impact.

Now try this. Move your left foot off the line and open up your stance. Notice the loss of stability. See Figures 41 and 42.

Figure 41: *Stance that is too open.*

Figure 42: *Boxing stance that is too wide, with palm down.*

Now try narrowing your stance, with your right toe aligned with your left toe. Now your stance is too narrow. See Figures 43 and 44. Notice how much less stable this feels.

Figure 43: *Stance that is too closed.*

Figure 44: *Apply force to narrow boxing stance and note feeling at impact.*

Now let's return to the JKD stance. Line up your feet correctly, with the toe of your front foot lined up with the arch of your rear foot. Raise your left heel slightly, as Nadi would instruct you to do. Remember that this is the piston of the entire fighting machine! As your partner hits your fist, you should feel a noticeable difference from our original Wing Chun stance. You should feel much more balanced, able to absorb most of the blow without any stress on joints or other body parts.

We still have one final step. Rotate your hips, enabling full shoulder extension. This is the point of impact for a properly thrown JKD straight lead. Keep your center of gravity low. You should feel solid as a rock with virtually no impact from your partner's force. See Figure 45.

Figure 45: *Back to the JKD stance.*

Remember Newton's third law: When one object exerts a force on a second object, the second object exerts an equal but opposite force on the first. Apply this law to hitting the heavy bag. You hit the bag. The bag exerts an equal force back at you. Sometimes you don't land squarely, and that jarring effect you get is the bag sending equal but opposite force at you.

The whole idea of the JKD stance is to align yourself to receive the least amount of punishment coming back to you. When you send out your punch, you are in the best possible position to receive the equal but opposite returning force.

You are also sending out the most efficient and powerful punch possible. You are aligned in such a way as not to lose any power along the kinetic chain. In other words, you have no weak links, and because you are not losing any power along the way, you are sending everything in your opponent's direction.

This is one of the best arguments for the JKD stance, of course, but people often over-look the fact that proper technique in throwing a straight lead can keep you in the game, thanks to Newton's law. A properly thrown straight lead causes the least wear and tear on joints, tendons, ligaments, and so on. It's all a matter of putting science and precision into practice.[22]

Notes

[1] Bruce Lee, ed. John Little, *Jeet Kune Do: Bruce Lee's Commentaries on the Martial Way* (Boston: Tuttle Publishing, 1997), pp. 385–386.

[2] Ibid., pp. 51–53.

[3] Lee, ed. John Little, p. 186. Some have claimed that Bruce found it beneficial to adapt both a left and right lead stance, but this nowhere to be found in any of his writings. The emphasis has always been on the strong hand in front.

[4] James E. Loehr, *The New Toughness Training for Sports*, (New York: Penguin Books, 1995), p. 167.

[5] Aldo Nadi, *On Fencing*, (Bangor, ME: Laureate Press, 1994), p. 51.

[6] Lee, ed. John Little, *Jeet Kune Do: Bruce Lee's Commentaries on the Martial Way*, p. 193. More piston and trigger allusions can be found on page 186:

> The left heel is up and cocked, ready to pull the trigger. It is the piston.
> To be more agile
> For faster footwork and drive
> For more power in punching

[7] Nadi, *On Fencing*, p. 51.

[8] Lee, *Tao of Jeet Kune Do* (Santa Clarita, CA, Ohara Publications, Inc., 1975), p. 146.

[9] Edwin L. Haislet, *Boxing* (New York: A.S. Barnes & Noble Company, 1940), p. 2. Haislet's description of balance is almost a textbook definition emphasizing keeping the center of gravity within the base determined by foot position:

> The primary purpose of boxing is hitting. Therefore, the use of the fundamental position is to obtain the most favorable position for hitting. To hit effectively is to obtain the most favorable position for hitting. To hit effectively it is necessary to shift the weight constantly from one leg to the other. This means perfect control of body balance. Balance is the most important consideration of the fundamental position.

Balance is achieved only through correct body alignment. The feet, the legs, the trunk, the head are all important in creating and maintaining a balanced position. The arms are important only because they are the vehicles of body force. They only give expression to body force when the body is in proper alignment. A position of the hands and arms, which facilitates easy body expression is important. The foot position is the most important. The foot position is the most important phase of balance. Keeping the feet in proper relation to each other as well as to the body helps to maintain correct body alignment.

[10] Lee, ed. John Little, *Jeet Kune Do: Bruce Lee's Commentaries on the Martial Way*, p. 186.

[11] Nadi, *On Fencing*, p. 51.

[12] *Knowing Is Not Enough: The Official Newsletter of The Bruce Lee Educational Foundation.* (Vol. 3, No. 3, ISSN: 1033-1325, pp 14–17).

[13] Jack Dempsey, *Championship Fighting: Explosive Punching and Aggressive Defence* (New York: Prentice Hall, Inc., 1950), p. 34. Dempsey's description of the Power Line:

> *The power line runs from either shoulder—straight down the length of the arm—to the* FIST KNUCKLE OF THE LITTLE FINGER, *when the fist is doubled. Remember: The power line ends in the first knuckle of the little finger on either hand. Gaze upon your "pinky" with new respect. You might call that pinky knuckle the exit of your power line—the muzzle of your cannon. You'll understand the power line if you feel it out.*

[14] Lee, *Tao of Jeet Kune Do*, p. 53.

[15] Ibid., p. 33. The exact quote that Bruce referenced can be found in Haislet's book—see note 16 below.

[16] Haislet, *Boxing*, p. 4. Haislet on the advantages of hip rotation and presenting a smaller target:

> *The one important thing about the trunk is that it should form a straight line with the leading leg.* As the leading foot and leg are turned inward the body rotates in the same direction, which presents a narrow target to the opponent. If, however, the leading foot and leg are rotated outward, the body is squared toward the opponent, presenting a large target. For defensive purposes, the narrow target is advantageous, while the square position lends itself better to some attacks.

[17] Michael A. Clark and Rodney J. Corn, *NASM Optimum Performance Training for the Fitness Professional* (Calabasas: National Academy of Sports Medicine, 2001), p. 45.

[18] Ibid., 356-357.

[19] Lee, *Tao of Jeet Kune Do*, p. 51.

[20] Ibid., p. 154.

[21] Lee, ed. John Little, *Jeet Kune Do: Bruce Lee's Commentaries on the Martial Way*, pp. 385-386.

[22] See William Cheung and Ted Wong, *Wing Chun Kung Fu/Jeet Kune Do: A Comparison Vol. 1* (Santa Clarita, CA: Ohara Publications, Inc., 1990), p. 19, for illustrations of Ted Wong's stance.

MECHANICS OF THE STRAIGHT LEAD

Now that you know how to construct the proper JKD stance, it's time to move on to the actual mechanics that set the straight lead into motion. To truly understand those mechanics, we'll have to review some elementary physics along the way.

Over the years, I've come to realize what a technical marvel the straight lead is. In investigating the disciplines of biomechanics, physics, and the history of fighting science, Bruce Lee was ahead of his time, and judging from the way that many people still throw their punches, he's still light years ahead. Indeed, the straight lead is a beautiful example of scientific application—the laws of physics set into poetic motion.

PRINCIPLES BEHIND THE STRAIGHT LEAD

As we dive into this chapter on mechanics, always keep in mind what Bruce listed as "the essential qualities of the lead punch":

- Economy of form
- Accuracy
- Speed
- Explosive power[1]

GREATER THAN THE SUM OF ITS PARTS

You'll also want to keep in mind that the end force production of the straight lead is greater than the sum of its parts. The idea is that less movement equals less time and energy. You never want any single body part to travel more than it has to. For example, if you throw an arm punch, not only will you have less power without your body weight behind it, but you'll also be slower, not to mention more fatigued. If you're only using one set of muscles, they're going to get tired a lot faster than if you recruit other muscles to help out.

That's why the feet and hips are so important in the straight lead. Your arm can only move so fast by itself. But if the hand covers some distance and your feet also cover distance, you'll get there a lot faster. And as you'll see shortly, rotating the hips will give you even more acceleration, and more acceleration means additional force.

THE KINETIC CHAIN

The principle that the force behind a punch should be greater than the sum of its parts is what the world of biomechanics refers to as the *kinetic chain*. What I call the "science of how to best throw your weight around" is nothing new to the world of sports, and the sequence of how to best accomplish this is what we call the kinetic chain. The kinetic chain is the coordinated activation of body segments in such a way as to generate maximum velocity, force, or some other desired outcome. See Figure 46.

This principle can be applied to any athletic technique: the football pass, a golf swing, a baseball pitch, a volleyball serve, soccer's instep kick, and, yes, the straight lead.

Applied to the straight lead, the purpose of the kinetic chain is to place the end segment, the hand, in the best position to generate optimum velocity, which in turn, generates maximum force. The correct body segment activation results in generation of a force that is greater than the sum of its parts. This is why we discourage "arm punching." It's an inefficient way of throwing a punch. It's slower and generates minimal force. Your arm can only generate so much force by itself. But by pushing from the ground up and rotating the trunk, you are able to send all of your body weight behind your arm. This is true of mechanics in all sports.

THE SEQUENCE

When it comes to executing punches and kicks, JKD truly is the science of how to best throw your weight around. Punches should be, as Bruce noted, "Not just arm power—strike with correct timing of foot, waist, and hip, shoulder, and wrist motion."[2]

Figure 46: *There's a lot more to hook punches than just arm power.*

Note the phrase "correct timing." To avoid mere arm punching, we must follow an intricate sequence of steps in throwing the straight lead. Essentially, the straight lead can be thought of as six specific steps in the following order:

1. The hand

2. The push-off

3. Hip rotation and shoulder extension

4. Contact with target

5. Landing of front foot

6. Landing of rear foot and hand retraction

Now let's take a closer look at each of these steps. At times, we will have to break them up, because certain steps overlap each other.

STEP ONE: HAND BEFORE FOOT, ALWAYS

The straight lead is the most difficult technique in JKD, and, fittingly, the very first motion of this punch is the most difficult step to master. The hand must move before anything else, which is a very unnatural motion. When we run, for example, we are used to synchronization of our arms and legs. This is not the case with the straight lead.[3]

The concept of *"hand before foot"* has its roots in fencing. Bruce took his cues from Nadi who wrote, "The arm must extend before the right foot moves for the execution of the lunge—a rule that must remain engraved in your mind forever. *Hand before foot, always."*[4] You'll find Bruce's referencing of Nadi in the *Tao of Jeet Kune Do:* "One important point: In all hand techniques, the hand moves first, preceding the foot. Keep this in mind—*hand before foot*—always.[5]

There are several reasons for Nadi's insistence. The first is a matter of speed. You will always be able to move your hand and arm faster than your legs or trunk, resulting in a punch that will reach its target sooner. See Figures 47 and 48.

Figure 47: *Starting point from stance.*

This would be a good time to introduce *Newton's first law of motion,* which states that an object at rest or moving uniformly at the same speed, in a straight line will continue in that state unless forces act upon it. In JKD, when we are at rest in the stance, we are in a state of inertia. Muscular forces cause us to move our hands and feet, setting us into motion and enabling us to overcome inertia.

Figure 48: *The lead hand should already be in motion before the feet move.*

Newton's second law of motion says that an object's acceleration is directly proportional to the force acting on it and is inversely proportional to its mass. In other words, the less an object's mass, the easier it is to accelerate that object. So, if we're in the JKD stance at rest, in a state of inertia, it will be much easier for us to overcome inertia and accelerate our hand, which has less mass than our larger body parts—our trunk or legs.

Newton's second law is expressed by the following equation:

$$force = mass \times acceleration$$

This is a central principle of JKD. At 5'7" and anywhere between 126 and 143 pounds, Bruce Lee was able to generate more force in his punches and kicks than men of much greater weight and body mass. The equation explains how Bruce made up for his lack in stature with the ability to accelerate, to change his speed from zero to greased lightning in very little time.

While for beginners, "Hand before Foot" may feel awkward and counterproductive, it is actually a key element in generating force for the straight lead. Greater acceleration obviously also means a better chance of hitting an opponent. Hand before foot also makes the JKD jab highly deceptive. If only the hand moves initially, it is already halfway to the target before it can be detected. Thwack! Your opponent's head has already snapped back before he or she has even realized you've gotten a shot off. The slightest movement of the trunk or legs—both made telegraphic by their larger size, greater visibility, and decreased capacity for acceleration—before the hand has initiated the punch will give you away.

While Hand before Foot is an essential component of the straight lead, attempting to master it can be maddening. We are accustomed to moving hand *with* foot, as in walking and running. In the beginning, you may want to walk through the straight lead moving your hand simultaneously with your feet, gradually training your lead hand to move ever so slightly before your feet. Use a mirror for visual feedback. As you practice, start out slowly, taking time to note how the correct sequence feels. Executing techniques in JKD, like any physical endeavor, is kinesthetic. Be patient. Like everything else, it's only a matter of neuromuscular programming.

BE NONTELEGRAPHIC

The straight lead is especially dangerous because of its *nontelegraphic* properties. I've already mentioned the advantage of using the lead hand because åΩof its proximity to the target. This is only an advantage, though, if it is executed properly. You shoot out your fist straight as an arrow from wherever it is and return the hand along the exact same path. In remaining consistent with the roots of JKD, Bruce wrote, "The punch should, and this applies to all punches and kicks, start from the ready stance without any unnecessary motions."[6] This may sound like common sense, but Dempsey seemed to think that being nontelegraphic was a point worth emphasizing repeatedly.[7] As always, streamlining your punches from start to finish makes them harder to read and gives them more speed and force.

STEP TWO: THE PUSH-OFF

Following the fist by mere milliseconds are the feet. This is the *push-off* mentioned in the chapter on footwork. If a large part of JKD is the science of how to best throw one's weight around, the push-off is what sets that weight into motion. You'll find no description of the push-off more eloquent than Nadi's.

> Raising the left heel ever so little, you cock the leg ready to pull the trigger and go into action. You take full advantage of one of the mightiest springs in all creation, the arch of the foot, which in the lunge releases its tremendous power through the pressure exerted on the ground by the ball of the foot itself.[8]

Sounds a bit dramatic, doesn't it? The importance, though, of the left leg, and more specifically, that resilient little left arch in JKD cannot be overemphasized. The left arch is what initiates the push-off. It determines how fast you can fire off a punch and the force with which you will fire.

There are a few things to remember that have already been addressed in the stance chapter. One, you want to feel all the weight on the inside of your legs. That's where the potential energy should be. More specifically, all the weight, tension, and potential energy should be directed toward and concentrated in the ball of your left foot. Going back to Newton's third law, the force you exert on the ground exerts an equal and opposite force up through your foot. This is how you are pushed off the ground. In biomechanics we call this *ground reaction force.*[9]

If the pressure you exert is dissipated and not concentrated—if, for example, some of your weight is rolling to the outside of the left (rear) leg or foot, you are going to have extra inertia to overcome on the take-off. It'll slow you down. See Figure 49.

Figure 49: *Part 1 of the push-off: launching off the left foot.*

Two, you want to have a controlled push-off. Again, Bruce emphasized small, controlled steps. You never want to sacrifice distance for balance. Keep in mind that you always want to retain the integrity of the stance. You are essentially moving from point A to point B without upsetting the on-guard position.

Also remember that the push-off is a take-off. You are unleashing all that potential energy stored in your left leg. Note the power to which Nadi referred and the "explosive" power described by Jack Dempsey, and later, Bruce.

In the same way that we accelerate the lead hand, we want to accelerate our entire body weight to generate power. To do so, intensity and explosiveness are required, starting from the ground.

A Slight Lean: Cheating Inertia

Before we move on to hip rotation it's important to note that there's more to the push-off than just the actual push. Remember from Newton's first law, we need to overcome inertia in order to launch into the straight lead. In general, your weight is distributed 50-50 between your right and left leg. But when you are poised to throw a straight lead, you actually cheat inertia a little by shifting your weight ever so slightly to the lead leg, and you'll require less force to propel your body weight into the punch.

The shift is almost imperceptible. There is a slight turn at the left hip, and with this turn comes a tiny extension of the left knee. The left heel will be raised an additional inch or two. This opens up the stance and shifts the weight forward. Again, it is almost imperceptible, but with your weight already shifted in the direction you plan to move, it will be a little easier to overcome inertia and propel your body forward. See Figures 50 through 53.

This tiny shift is like cocking a gun. You employ it only when you're just about ready to fire. Also note this shift is just enough to give you an edge over inertia but not so much as to upset your balance.

You'll find evidence for the slight lean in the *Tao of Jeet Kune Do* in which Bruce mentions maintaining a "slightly forward center of gravity."[10]

Figure 50: *Starting from the stance.*

Figure 51: *The slight lean. The left heel is slightly raised, causing your weight to shift forward.*

Figure 52: *Starting position.*

Figure 53: *When you lean forward, you'll also turn slightly to your right.*
This slightly opens the stance and gives you more room for hip rotation.

WAYS TO DIRECT MOTION

Now would be a good time to discuss the three directions of motion involved in throwing any punch. First, we have *linear horizontal motion*, motion along a straight-line path. In JKD, this means moving forward or backward. The second direction is *linear vertical motion*—in the simplest terms, up and down relative to the earth's surface. Jumping up and down is an example of vertical motion. So is the legwork involved in throwing an uppercut. Finally, we have *rotational motion*, defined as circular movement about an axis. Think of a door swinging on a hinge.

We'll come back to the push-off, directions of motion, and the importance of a correctly timed landing shortly. But before we do that, we need to discuss hip rotation and shoulder extension.

STEP THREE: HIP ROTATION AND SHOULDER EXTENSION

For you to understand the third step in throwing a straight lead, I'll need to describe a particular type of motion that physicists call *projectile motion*. A projectile is defined as any object that moves through the air or through space, acted on only by gravity.[11] If we were to shoot an arrow straight ahead, it would follow a curved path downward and would eventually hit the ground. This downward motion is a result of gravity, which exerts vertical force downward on the arrow. If it weren't for gravity, the arrow would continue forever in a straight path. Because of gravity, however, it is actually moving in two directions—straight ahead in a horizontal path and downward toward the earth's surface. As it is being pulled toward the ground, the speed at which it travels horizontally is slowed. When you throw the straight lead, your body follows a similar curved path. The trajectory of any projectile is shown in Figure 54.

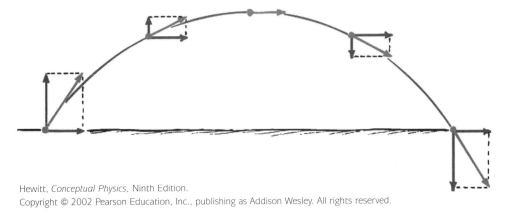

Figure 54: *Trajectory of projectile motion.*

When throwing a straight lead, rotation of the hip helps to compensate for this effect of gravity. First, it enables you to increase your acceleration toward the target. Once you have thrown out your lead hand and pushed off the ground, gravity is going to slow you down as it drags you toward the ground. But this isn't what we want! To generate the most force, you need to continue to accelerate.

To achieve this, you rotate your torso. This is where Ted Wong uses the analogy of a wave. If you've ever watched waves at the beach, you'll notice a wave might start out by itself and then join another. And that bigger wave, which was originally two, might join yet another and so on. You'll also notice that that one big wave continues to pick up speed as it approaches the beach. Each smaller one brings a momentum and acceleration of its own, adding to the larger wave's acceleration. That gnarly bombora gathers in speed with each smaller wave it picks up until it eventually crashes onto the shore.[12]

This is the principle behind the sequence of the straight lead. We want to pick up speed with each step. First, the hand shoots out. Then we push off. In the second half of the push-off, as we are being dragged down by gravity, a quick turn of the hips allows us to gather speed just before we make contact with the target.

Acceleration isn't the only benefit of hip rotation. One of the key principles of JKD is that in any punch or kick, you want your hips to move toward the target so that, at impact, the hip is pointing toward it. This has to do, again, with the science of how to best throw your weight around. Most of your weight is located in your trunk. Rotate your trunk, and you're able to direct most of your body weight into a punch.

The principle is true of just about any sport. In baseball, the force of your swing depends largely on the torque you generate with your hips. As tennis technique has become more sophisticated, players have switched from a closed forehand stance to an open stance to allow for greater hip rotation. In Joe Montana's *Art and Magic of Quarterbacking*, he discusses how he uses his body to throw passes as opposed to just using his arm. He goes on to explain how proper mechanics saved his arm and lengthened his career.[13] The same goes for JKD. We *never* want to arm-punch. As Dempsey emphasized throughout his book, the key to forceful punches is knowing how to use your body weight.

As shown in the chapter on the stance, rotation of the hips also puts us in the best alignment to absorb forces coming back to us, again, saving some wear and tear on our joints. And if that weren't enough, that little extra hip turn gives us a few critical inches of extended reach.

You'll want to "put your shoulder" into the punch when you rotate your hips. Fully extend at the shoulder, but beware. Do not add extra linear reach by straightening your legs. This is a very common mistake. People tend to think that because the lead punch is directed linearly toward the target, all the power must come from linear mechanisms. Wrong. The rotation of your trunk is critical to generating force. The linear portion of the punch is mainly controlled by extension of the hand and the push-off.[14] See Figures 55 and 56.

Figure 55: *Do not try to add power by straightening your knee and reaching forward. When your torso overtakes your knee, you lose balance and leverage.*

Figure 56: *Correct hip rotation and shoulder extension. The center of gravity is kept low and is well within the boundaries determined by both feet.*

So when rotating your hips and extending the shoulder, make sure you maintain the integrity of your stance. Keep your center of gravity low, and maintain the bend and give in your knees. A trick I like to use is to look at the stripes on my pants. The stripes should turn while your legs remain bent at the knees. Other than a slight forward lean, your torso does not move forward. See Figures 57 and 58.

Figure 57: *Starting position. Note where my pant stripes are.*

Figure 58: *Rotation with shoulder and arm extension. My pant stripes should now be facing the target, but at the same time, my torso never overtakes my front knee.*

Rotational motion plays a much larger part in other punches, like the hook, but it is a critical element in throwing all punches, including an effective straight lead.

STEP FOUR: WE HAVE CONTACT! THE STRAIGHT LEAD AT IMPACT

From the chapter on the stance, you already know about the power line and why it's so important to land with the bottom three knuckles at impact. You'll not only add more force to your punches, but you'll also greatly reduce the risk of hand and wrist injuries. A few things you need to keep in mind at the very moment of impact are distance, accuracy, and follow-through.

LEVERAGE

Knowing how to throw a straight lead is of little use if we aren't in the proper position. Obviously, if we're too far from the target, we can't reach it. Less obvious is that being too close is almost as bad. If you jam yourself, you lose leverage. As an example, consider the bench press. Lifting early into a single rep is harder than lifting the last 3–4 inches. As you straighten your arms for those last few inches, you have the most leverage. The same is true of the straight lead. You'll want to have about 3–4 inches left to extend at the elbow when your fist actually touches the target. This is where you will have the most leverage, and you want that point to be at the very moment you make contact. To maximize leverage, then, you need to maintain proper distance from the target. See Figures 59 and 60.

Figure 59: *Correct arm position at impact allows optimal leverage.*

Figure 60: *You should have just enough bend in your arm at impact to allow for a follow-through of about 3 inches past the target.*

ACCURACY

Up to this point, we've initiated the straight lead by shooting the hand out before moving our feet. We've exploded off the ground with the push-off. We've increased the speed of our hand and launched our body weight into the punch by rotating our trunk and shoulders, and we've perfectly judged our distance. But all of this is worth very little if we miss the target. To throw an effective punch, you must direct all of your speed, energy, form, alignment, and body weight toward one little point that culminates at those bottom three knuckles of your hand.

This is where focus mitt drills are invaluable. Unlike the heavy bag, when it comes to accuracy, the focus mitts don't lie. You'll want to land squarely on that little dot—it's there for a reason—every time. No skidding off the mitt. No wobbling mitts. You'll know when you land a good one. You'll *feel* it. Of course, you won't want your eyes riveted to a potential target all the time. But you do want to focus your eyes like a laser on the target during those milliseconds prior to impact.

Likewise, your hand should be completely relaxed right up to the moment before hitting the target. Being unnecessarily tense wastes energy and slows you down. Think about it. Once you see the target, you have to overcome that tension and relax your muscles first, so that you can move them. You can eliminate this step by being relaxed in the first place. Easier said than done, I know. Just don't forget to work on it.

As for fist clenching, remember that it doesn't occur until just before impact.[15] As is always the case—muscles should only be activated when they are needed. Otherwise, you waste energy and restrict your ability to move quickly.

FOLLOW-THROUGH

The final stage of making contact with a target is follow-through. Here, Bruce was influenced by Haislet:

> A blow is never hit at a mark. It is driven through a mark. Follow-through is just
> as important in fighting as it is in any other sport and follow-through can only
> be obtained by punching through and beyond the point of attack.[16]

Throwing a football, baseball, shot put, or frisbee. The golf swing. Tennis serve, backhand, forehand. They all end with follow-through. The straight lead is no different. Always keep in mind that you'll want to punch through the target about 3–4 inches past the point of contact.

This is where momentum comes into play. I'll define and discuss momentum in more detail in the next section. For now, just know that we don't want to decrease our momentum *before* contact. We want to maximize use of that body weight at the point of contact. Your momentum will carry you into follow-through.

STEP FIVE: LANDING OF THE FRONT FOOT

WHAT GOES UP MUST COME DOWN: THE SECOND HALF OF THE PUSH-OFF

Rotation of the hips is considered the final step before contact with the target, but as this occurs, you will be in mid-air, on your way back down to the ground in the second half of the push-off.

Recall that the first half of the push-off sets the body in two of these directions—horizontally (linear) and vertically (upward). The horizontally linear aspect of the push-off is very much like a fencer's lunge, propelling the body forward in the direction of the target. Intuitively, this makes sense. An object coming toward us in a straight line, say a fist, carries a certain force with it, and we are going to get out of its way!

Less well understood, however, is the role that vertical motion plays in the straight lead and how the push-off makes this vertical motion possible. Again, we turn to science—and, again, the science of *projectile motion*. Remember, a projectile is defined as any object that moves through the air or through space, acted on only by gravity. Recall the curved path of a cannonball as it is pulled toward the earth's surface by gravity.

To compensate for this gravitational effect, we sometimes upwardly launch projectiles as in the case of aiming a cannonball or throwing a javelin. Note that the more upwardly a projectile is launched, the less horizontal distance it can cover. So it's important to find the most effective vertical launch for the push-off. In this case, it is just a slightly upward launch. More than that, and you will sacrifice the linear distance you are able to cover.

In the case of the push-off, your body is essentially a projectile as your left leg launches you both in a linear and upward direction. For practical purposes, we must launch ourselves slightly upward because merely moving in a linear direction would mean that we would have to slide toward our opponent, and the friction of the ground would slow us down, reducing our acceleration, and, thus, force—not to mention severely scuffing our shoes.

But the push-off serves a less obvious purpose in that it is an additional means of generating force for the straight lead. If the initial half of the push-off, the launch, comes from Nadi and the fencing lunge, the latter half of the push-off, the landing, has its roots in old-time fistic science.

THE FALLING STEP

While you won't find many direct Jack Dempsey quotes in the *Tao of Jeet Kune Do* or *Bruce Lee's Commentaries on the Martial Way*, Dempsey's influence on the straight lead was enormous—from the thumbs up fist, three-knuckle landing, and power line to the hand-before-foot landing and falling step. In his own copy of Dempsey's *Championship Fighting: Explosive Punching and Aggressive Defence*, Bruce had marked entire passages that would become major influences on Jeet Kune Do.[17]

One of Dempsey's main arguments was that taking advantage of body mass and gravity could increase punching force. Because of gravity, what goes up must come down. And so with the push-off: once you have launched yourself slightly upward, you must eventually come down. This is the principle behind the falling step.

Remember the equation for force production is expressed as:

$$\text{force} = \text{mass} \times \text{acceleration}$$

Powerful punches, then, are the product of setting your body weight into "fast motion"—in other words, accelerating body mass. In a passage heavily underlined by Bruce Lee, Dempsey stated:

> There are four ways of setting the body-weight in motion for punching: (1) falling forward; (2) springing forward; (3) whirling the shoulders by means of the powerful back muscles, assisted by shifting weight from one leg to the other, and (4) by surging upwards, as in delivering uppercuts. Every punch combines at least two of those motion-methods.[18]

What Dempsey has described here are the three directions of motion discussed earlier. Falling forward would be a combination of vertical and linear motion. Springing forward would be linear. "Whirling" is a rotational motion. And "surging upwards" is movement in a vertical direction.

Dempsey argued that every punch combines at least two of these motions. Part of what makes the straight lead so difficult is that it involves all of them. I will discuss "whirling," or rotational motion, later, but let's get back to the push-off. I've already noted that the push-off is a combination of "surging upwards" and "springing forward." What we haven't discussed is what Dempsey listed as the first method of setting the body in motion, "falling forward." You might say that the first half of the JKD push-off—moving upward and forward—is Nadi influenced, and the second half of the push-off—moving downward and forward—comes from Dempsey.

Remember our discussion of projectile motion and the curved path a projectile must take as it is acted on by gravity? The upward launch of the push-off is the first half of that curved path. As a projectile approaches the ground, the second half of that curved path is what Dempsey referred to as "the falling step."

Essentially, what we are doing with the falling step is making gravity work for us. If gravity is going to exert a force on us anyway, why not use that extra force and redirect it toward our target? Dempsey dedicated an entire chapter to illustrating the falling step, which he called "the gem movement of straight punching." Actually, the falling step at the end of the push-off is very much like walking. Walking is really a series of falls. You lift one foot up and are unstable for a moment until your foot hits the ground. Gravity is what compels you to put your foot on the ground, and if you didn't put that foot down, you'd be doing a whole lot of stumbling.[19]

The difference between walking and punching is that by extending your fist, you focus much of that gravitational force toward the target. So, the next step is to harness that gravitational force and channel it into your punches. See Figure 61.

Figure 61: *The straight lead at impact. I've made contact with the target while still in the air. This way, I redirect gravity's downward pull into the punch and not into the ground. My arm is bent just enough to allow for 3–4 inches of follow-through. This is also the first part of the three-point landing.*

REDIRECTING DOWNWARD FORCE

As you may recall from high school physics, the *velocity* of an object has both magnitude and *direction*. In physics, these two qualities are represented in diagrams by arrows called *vectors*. I don't want to go into too much detail regarding vectors here, so we'll just cover the basics. As you already know, an object may travel along a path comprising more than one direction. In the case of coming down from the push-off, we would be traveling both toward the target and toward the ground. A separate vector would represent each direction. The sum of two or more vectors is called their *resultant*.

The diagram below illustrates how vectors represent the direction of a projectile. At the beginning of the curve, the projectile is moving both upward and horizontally. The diagonal vector is the resultant. At the end of the curve, the projectile is moving both downward and horizontally. Again, the diagonal vector is the resultant. See Figure 62.

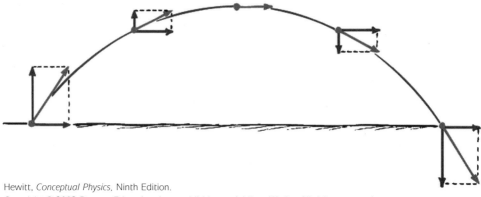

Figure 62: *Projectile trajectory and its constituent vectors.*

To determine the resultant of two vectors that aren't acting in the same or opposite direction, we use the *parallelogram rule* by applying the good ol' Pythagorean theorem expressed as:

$$R = \sqrt{(V^2 + H^2)}$$

To use a parallelogram, we take the sum of the squares of the vertical and horizontal vectors. Then we take the square root of this sum, which tells us what the diagonal vector is. For you geometry whizzes, yes, that's the hypotenuse. See Figure 63.

Figure 63: *Finding the resultant.*

Enough math? Don't worry. There won't be a pop quiz. Just keep these concepts in mind, though, as you try to master the straight lead. In terms of throwing a punch, let's look at how vectors are involved. During that second half of the push-off, you are traveling in two directions—linearly toward the target and vertically downward toward the earth. The resultant is the force you bring toward the target.

The concept of vectors is more easily understood in less abstract terms in Dempsey's example of a boy sledding down a slope. The sled is actually moving in two directions—downward as it is pulled to the earth by gravity and linearly. This is because the slope is at an angle, down a slope. At the bottom of the hill, however, all that downward force is redirected linearly, and the sled moves with increased speed on level ground.[20]

This is exactly what happens when we relay our body weight to a target with the straight punch. As we return to the ground after pushing off, we are also shooting out the lead hand. Because the push-off involves some upward vertical motion, the landing, in turn, involves some downward vertical motion due to gravity. That downward force of our body weight being pulled to the earth by gravity must be transferred to the target *before* we actually touch the ground. By doing so, we are able to redirect more of that downward force and use it to our advantage. See Figure 64.

Figure 64: *Follow-through and landing.*

STEP SIX: CONTACT AND RETRACTING THE HAND

In many martial arts, a punch ends once it lands the target, but this is not the case in Jeet Kune Do, where retraction of the hand is every bit as important as launching the hand from the on-guard stance. To understand why, once again, we'll turn to the laws of physics.

MOMENTUM AND IMPULSE

Recall Newton's first law of inertia: an object at rest or in motion in a straight line at a constant speed will continue in that state unless acted upon by a force. We define *momentum* as inertia in motion—an object traveling in a straight line at a constant speed. The equation for momentum is:

$$\text{momentum} = \text{mass} \times \text{velocity}$$

Also remember from the study of vectors that we define velocity as speed and direction. From the equation for momentum, we know that a small object, such as a bullet, can have tremendous momentum because when fired from a gun, it travels at an incredibly high speed. Conversely, a large object, such as a boulder, may have no momentum if it is at rest. Roll that boulder down a steep hill, though, and it will have quite a bit of momentum because of its velocity rolling down the hill.

Now let's consider another scenario in which we have an object whose mass remains the same but changes in velocity. This happens all the time. We have a golf ball at rest. Whack it with a five iron, and it changes its velocity—its speed and/or direction changes. Obviously, the object's momentum has changed because momentum is a function of velocity.

But there's something else we might want to measure—the time it takes to cause a change in momentum. And what causes a change in momentum? Remember momentum is a state of inertia, and to overcome inertia, we must apply force. The product of force and the time during which that force is applied to an object is called *impulse*. Mathematically, it is expressed as:

$$\text{impulse} = \text{force} \times \text{time}$$

Something to consider when discussing impulse is that the same impulse is always required to bring an object to rest (decrease momentum). What may vary, though, are the force and time. Let's consider the difference between rolling with a punch and running into one. When we roll with a punch, we increase the time over which force is applied, and as a result, the force or impact is decreased. If we run into a punch, the time it takes to change that fist's momentum to zero with our face is greatly decreased. Therefore, from the equation, we know the force is increased. That's why we roll away from punches instead of running into them.

Let's try another example. Consider the difference between fight gloves and training gloves. We all know that we'd rather face someone wearing training gloves. We feel less of our opponent's punches. Why? Training gloves are more heavily padded than fight gloves. The extra padding extends the length of time it takes our face to stop a punch. That fist has to wade through all that padding first. More time means less force. If we're facing fight gloves, though, we don't have that extra protection. A stiffer glove means less impact time. Our face brings that fist to a halt instantly. Not pretty.

SNAPPING AND JKD

So, what does all of this have to do with the final step in throwing a straight lead? Retracting the hand is obviously important because it gets us back into position to throw the next punch. But what isn't commonly understood is that *how* you retract that hand can greatly contribute to the damage you do.

From our discussion about impulse, you already know that the force of your fist will be much greater when the time of contact with a target is very short. The momentum of your fist is decreased considerably when you hit, for example, a focus mitt. And the less time your fist is in contact with that focus mitt, the greater the force of impact. A similar example is that of catching a baseball. If you move your hand forward to meet the ball, it's going to hurt a lot more than if you move your hand back as your glove makes contact with the ball. The impulse required to decrease the baseball's momentum remains the same. But increasing the time the force of the ball is applied to your glove decreases the force.

Now remember that so far we've discussed bringing objects in motion to rest by decreasing momentum. Also remember that velocity is determined by both speed and *direction*. What would happen if you actually changed direction of your fist by bouncing off the focus mitt and retracting the hand?

By changing the direction of your hand, you actually increase the impulse, thereby increasing the force required to change direction. Think about it. Stopping your fist requires a certain impulse. *Changing* direction after stopping your fist actually requires additional impulse. And if the time of contact, or time during which you apply force, is kept to a minimum, the force at impact will be even greater.

This is why Bruce always stressed the importance of "snappiness" to punches and kicks. It's not just that snapping your hand back into the stance puts you into better position to get the next shot off. It does. But snapping at the end of a punch allows you to retract your hand more quickly, allowing you to snap or bounce, and bouncing off a target, because of what we know about impulse, will give much more force to your punches.

This isn't to say that you don't "go through" the target as discussed in the previous section on making contact with the target. Penetrating the target is a very important part of doing damage with the straight lead. As Bruce wrote, "All punches should end with a snap several inches behind the target. Thus, you punch *through* the opponent yet end the punch with a snap."[21]

You *must* go through the target. But our arms are only so long. At some point, you will have to decrease your momentum to stop your hand. The faster you reverse direction and bring your hand back after it has stopped, though, the more forceful the impact as compared to the impact if you'd just let your hand dangle out there and then slowly retracted it. Snapping your punches is the difference between a devastating blow and an innocuous push.

THE MECHANICS OF RETRACTING THE HAND

We know that minimizing the time of contact with a target and then retracting the hand swiftly greatly increases force. But how do we go about doing that?

One of the most common mistakes when it comes to retracting is dropping the hand once it's hit the target. The reason we don't want to do this is simple. The shortest distance between two points is a straight line. In *Boxing*, Edwin Haislet stressed, "The arm must travel a straight line and return in a straight line."[22] If we drop our hand, we are actually moving in a circular motion, and this slows us down. The hand will have to travel a further distance to get back into position. Not only will you lose the snap that comes from snapping your hand back in a straight line, you will also lose precious time. You will never be able to fire effective double and triple jabs this way. Nor will you be ready to get any shot off if you are still out of position because of a slow retraction.

Remember, everything begins and ends with the stance. You want to get back as soon as possible to on-guard. If anything, your right hand should retract faster than it shoots out.

Dropping the hand on its way back to the on-guard position also significantly reduces your punch's efficacy at impact. Instead of directing all your force at and through the target, you will skid off the focus mitt. Hence, the name *focus* mitt. You want to focus all of your punch toward the target. You dissipate some of that force when you drop your hand. Skidding off the mitt splinters that force and increases the time of contact with the target, which as you'll recall from the discussion of impulse, decreases the damage your punch will cause.

The second most common mistake made when getting back into position is analogous to the pitfalls of arm punching. Remember the kinetic chain. You will be much faster and less fatigued if you avoid overtaxing any single body part. A very common problem is failure to rotate the hips when retracting the hand. If your arm covers only half the distance and your rotating hips cover the other half, you will be twice as fast than if you were to move only your arm.

THE THREE-POINT LANDING

The final step in executing the straight lead is what Ted Wong refers to as the three-point landing. Believe it or not, if there is a segment of the straight lead that might be called "easy," this is it, for if you have performed all the other steps perfectly and in their correct sequence, this final step literally should fall into place.

The first point of the three-point landing should be your fist on the target. You never want either the lead or rear foot to hit the ground before your hand lands the target. Why? Remember from the discussion of vectors and projectile motion that you want to take advantage of the downward gravitational force acting on your body mass. Also recall Dempsey's explanation of redirecting the sled horizontally at the bottom of the slope.

What you're doing by hitting the target before your front foot hits the ground is taking advantage of the second, downward half of projectile motion and redirecting the force of your body weight toward the target. If your foot lands before you hit the target, all that force goes into the ground and is wasted.

Regarding the mechanics of the front foot landing, you'll want to land on the heel first and then let the rest of the foot touch the floor. This is to ensure a stable landing. Landing on your toes, for instance, will result in a loss of balance. Again, we want to maintain that potential energy on the inside portion of both legs which enables quicker, more explosive movement. See Figure 65.

Figure 65: *For maximum stability and control, the landing starts with the touching down of the front heel. This is part two of the three-point landing.*

Landing of the rear foot is the last of the three points. After initiating the push-off, the left leg gets a well-deserved rest and merely goes along for the ride. The hand hits the target, the lead foot rests heel first on the ground, and the rear foot follows. As your hand retracts and your front foot lands, the rear foot completes the return to the on-guard position. At the end of the punch, you should be right back in the stance, feet slightly wider than shoulders' width apart, with no adjustments, no matter how small, required to fire off another perfect straight. See Figure 66.

Figure 66: *Part three of the three-point landing: touching down with the back foot.*

DRAWING IN

If you've spent any time in a gym lately, you'll know that there's a lot of talk these days about something called "core training." The core refers to that part of the body that includes everything except the arms and legs. In anatomical terms, we call this the *lumbo-pelvic-hip complex.*

The core comprises two muscle sets. The first group makes up the movement system and includes superficial muscles that help move the ribs, arms, and legs. These muscles include the latissimus dorsi, erector spinae, iliopsoas, hamstrings, adductors, rectus abdominus, and external obliques.

The second group consists of stabilizers. These are deep muscles that connect the vertebrae of the lumbar spine, pelvis, and sacrum and include the transverse abdominus, internal oblique, lumbar multifidus, pelvic floor muscles, and diaphragm. These muscles do not actually produce movement, but all movement requires their recruitment. [23]

And this goes back to the earlier discussion of body feel. You cannot actually see the activation of the deep musculature of the core. You have to feel it. Trainers refer to this as the *"drawing-in" maneuver.* You will find references to it in many instructional sports books. Studies have shown that in healthy people, activation of core musculature occurs between 30 and 110 milliseconds before outer muscle activity. From golf swings and tennis serves to chest presses and lat pull-downs, activation of the core muscles is necessary for efficient force production. The straight lead is no exception.

Again, this is something that you cannot see. In the simplest terms, you might describe "drawing in" as a slight tensing of the muscles in the abdominal area just prior to making a move.

To practice it, take a deep breath. This activates the diaphragm, which works synergistically with the transverse abdominus. Your rib cage should not be elevated. Exhale. Now draw in your navel, but do not "suck in" your belly. Drawing in is a much subtler muscle activation than sucking in your gut, and it shouldn't appear as if you're sucking it in. You should be able to do this without movement of the trunk, shoulders, head, or spine. Remember you are preparing your body for movement by stabilizing your core. This is accomplished by drawing in, which activates the rectus abdominus and external obliques.[24]

Activation of the core is imperative, for it is the foundation of all movement. Even if the movement system—arms and legs—is capable of producing force in isolation, overall force production will be greatly diminished without a strong core foundation, for it is the core that provides internal stability. It is the stable foundation on which the movement system is built.

On a more important note, a strong core leads to fewer injuries. If the core is not adequately activated before the movement system, the spine is not stabilized, leaving it vulnerable to forces acting on the intervertebral discs and joints. A weak core and/or failure to activate core muscles are leading causes of back injuries.

Again, you need to *feel* the drawing-in maneuver. Drawing in, by the way, is very closely related to your mental state. That preparation of your body just prior to shooting straight should be in sync with your mental preparation. Every time you throw a punch, you should feel that tension in your abdominal area just before doing so. To throw a hard and fast straight right, you must first stabilize the core.

"THE LAST MOMENT OF ACCELERATION"

In discussing the sequence of straight lead mechanics, I've digressed to explain the underlying physics and biomechanics of each step and why they've been placed in this particular order. So, let's review the sequence one more time.

The mechanical steps of the straight lead occur in this particular order with the aim of culminating in the greatest possible hand acceleration at the point of impact.[25] See Figures 67 through 72.

Figure 67: *Starting position from the stance. There is a subtle forward lean to cheat inertia. The left heel is raised and the stance is slightly open just before launching into the straight.*

Figure 68: *The hand initiates because it will always move faster than— and will reach the target before—any other body part. The rest of the body will catch up. Here, my front hand has already advanced, but my feet have yet to cover any ground.*

Figure 69: *The push-off will propel your entire body in a vertical and linear direction, enabling you to cover distance. The vertical component allows you to take advantage of downward gravitational force as well.*

Figure 70: *Contact with the target should allow for 3–4 inches of follow-through behind the target for optimum leverage. Contact should be snappy— not pushy—to minimize impact time and maximize force.*

Figure 71: *The front foot lands only after the hand has landed so that gravitational forces are redirected toward the target and not wasted by their direction to the ground. Just prior to contact, hip rotation and shoulder extension add additional acceleration to compensate for gravity's pull on the body mass.*

Figure 72: *The landing of the rear foot naturally follows the landing of the front foot, while the hand retracts along the exact same straight path from which it came. This expedites the return to the on-guard position, facilitating the initiation of follow-up shots.*

STAYING WITH THE STRAIGHT

The sequence of the straight can be exceedingly frustrating to master, and at times, can seem hardly worth the trouble. But the rewards are well worth the effort, for the lead jab in JKD has a foundation rooted in a rich history of fighting science and the sound laws of physics.

Again, the straight lead evolved over thousands of years. Do not skip steps or settle for sloppy form or technique. There are scientific reasons for those steps. Once you have developed a certain degree of competency in performing them, their advantages will reveal themselves to you.[26]

Yes, you will be frustrated. At times you may wonder if you are getting lost in the minutiae of technical details. But keep in mind that the properly executed JKD straight lead is a flawless marriage of physicality and science and a kind of perfection worth striving for.

NOTES

[1] Bruce Lee, ed. John Little, *Jeet Kune Do: Bruce Lee's Commentaries on the Martial Way* (Boston: Tuttle Publishing, 1997), p. 213.

[2] Ibid., p. 211.

[3] Ibid., p. 253. According to Bruce:

The first requirement in advance is:

1. Psychological moment
2. Hand moves before foot

Your body must not be overreached

[4] Aldo Nadi, *On Fencing*, (Bangor, ME: Laureate Press, 1994), p. 89.

[5] Bruce Lee, *Tao of Jeet Kune Do* (Santa Clarita, CA, Ohara Publications, Inc., 1975), p. 97.

[6] Lee, ed. John Little, *Jeet Kune Do: Bruce Lee's Commentaries on the Martial Way*, p. 253.

[7] Jack Dempsey, *Championship Fighting: Explosive Punching and Aggressive Defence* (New York: Prentice Hall, Inc., 1950), pp. 33, 48. Bruce's emphasis on nontelegraphic punches is common sense but appears to have been heavily influenced by Dempsey, as well as Haislet. The following passage on being nontelegraphic was highlighted in Bruce's own copy of Dempsey's book:

Learn now and remember always that in fighting you cannot afford to give your body the luxury of a useless preliminary or preparatory movement before shooting a punch. In the first place, your target may be open for only a split second, and you must take advantage of that opening like a bolt of lightning. Secondly, preliminary movements are give-always—"telltales"—that treacherously betray to your opponent your next action." And: "Do not draw back—or "cock"—the relaxed left [lead] hand in a preparatory movement that you hope will give the punch more zing. Don't do that! You'll not only telegraph the blow, but you'll slow up and weaken the punch.

[8] Nadi, *On Fencing*, p. 51. You will find many of Bruce's comments on the left leg, particularly the piston and trigger references, come from this passage:

> The left leg is not just a prop. It is the spark plug, or better still the piston of the whole fencing machine. This leg provides a great deal of the power and speed that are needed for a correct, fast lunge. In preparation for this, the left heel should always be slightly off the floor (about half an inch). All fencing teachers will tell you to keep both feet constantly flat on the strip. I say—No.
>
> Raising the left heel ever so little, you cock the leg ready to pull the trigger and go into action. You take full advantage of one of the mightiest springs in all creation, the arch of the foot, which in the lunge releases its tremendous power through the pressure exerted on the ground by the ball of the foot itself.

[9] Michael A. Clark and Rodney J. Corn, *NASM Optimum Performance Training for the Fitness Professional* (Calabasas: National Academy of Sports Medicine, 2001), p. 49.

[10] Lee, *Tao of Jeet Kune Do*, p. 33.

[11] Paul G. Hewitt, *Conceptual Physics 9th Edition* (San Francisco: Addison Wesley, 2002), p. 774.

[12] Ted Wong with John Little, "Bruce Lee's Lead Punch: Ted Wong Explains Jun Fan Jeet Kune Do's Most Explosive Technique!" *Bruce Lee: The Official Publication & Voice of the Jun Fan Jeet Kune Do Nucleus*, June 2000, pp. 58–69.

[13] Joe Montana with Richard Weiner, *Joe Montana's Art and Magic of Quarterbacking* (New York: Henry Holt and Company, 1997), p. 51. Montana referred himself as a "body thrower," not an "arm thrower."

[14] Bruce Lee and M. Uyehara, *Bruce Lee's Fighting Method* (Burbank, CA: Ohara Publications, Inc., 1978), pp. 248-249. These are excellent photos of Bruce throwing the lead punch. Notice that he leans forward, but his center of gravity never overtakes his lead foot.

[15] Lee, ed. John Little, *Jeet Kune Do: Bruce Lee's Commentaries on the Martial Way*, p. 211.

[16] Ibid., p. 210. Compare to Edwin L. Haislet, *Boxing* (New York: A.S. Barnes & Noble Company, 1940), p. 16.

[17] Examples of those passages and where Bruce took special note can be found in *Knowing Is Not Enough: The Official Newsletter of The Bruce Lee Educational Foundation*, Vol. 3, No. 3, ISSN: 1033-1325, pp. 14–17.

[18] Dempsey, *Championship Fighting: Explosive Punching and Aggressive Defence*, p. 26.

[19] Ibid., pp. 31–33.

[20] Ibid., p. 29. Dempsey's explanation:

> In a sense, the boy and his sled are falling objects, like the baby. But the slope of the hill prevents then from falling straight down. Their fall is deflected to the angle of the hill. The direction of their weight-in-motion is on a slant. And when they reach the level plain at the bottom of the hill, they will continue to slide for a while. However, the direction of their slide on the plain—the direction of their weight-in-motion—will be straight out, at a right angle to the straight-down pull of gravity.

[21] Bruce Lee, ed. John Little, *The Tao of Gung Fu* (Boston: Tuttle Publishing, 1997), p. 211.

[22] Haislet, *Boxing*, p. 16.

[23] Clark and Corn, *NASM Optimum Performance Training for the Fitness Professional*, p. 104.

[24] Ibid., 106.

[25] Lee, *Tao of Jeet Kune Do*, p. 58. Bruce drew comparisons with the mechanics of other sports:

> An important aspect of this multiple action of acceleration is the introduction of each segment movement as late as possible in order to take full advantage of the peak acceleration of its fulcrum. The principle is to preserve the maximum acceleration up to the last instant of contact. Regardless of distance, the final phase of a movement should be the fastest.

[26] Nadi, *On Fencing*, p. 97. Nadi, ever the stickler for precise technique, had this to say:

> Even when you have mastered [an] almost uncanny mind-reading faculty, you can exploit it only if you succeed in developing perfect timing, faultless co-ordination, tremendous speed, and utter precision of point. Your initial step is to learn patiently the mechanical performance of all actions—this being the only way to acquire the aforementioned qualities. For to guess correctly the adversary's parries is of no avail unless you are able to execute perfectly the actions that deceive them. Therefore, those qualities will never be yours until you have become proficient in the proper technique of the art.

FOOTWORK

*"The Quality of a Man's Technique Depends
on What He Does with His Feet"*[1]

The subject of footwork is much too vast to cover adequately in one chapter and warrants its own entire volume, for as Nadi declared, "Footwork is the foundation of the fencer."[2] Indeed it is the foundation of all athletic and martial endeavors. It was Joe Montana's footwork that caught the eye of Bill Walsh for the 1979 NFL draft. Listen to John McEnroe's commentary. When he comes across a player he likes, the first things he raves about are "big, strong legs" and "great footwork." Andre Agassi told Charlie Rose that increased footwork precision has been key to his tennis longevity. Many believe Nadi's greatest strength was his footwork, and Sugar Ray Leonard[3] said that he learned much of his footwork by studying Bruce Lee's films.

Bruce himself said, "Footwork can beat any attack, and a properly maintained distance will baffle any skilled opponent."[4] If it means beating *any* attack, isn't it worth developing?

With so many elite athletes arguing the importance of footwork, it amazes me that it is so understudied, overlooked, and outright neglected. Martial artists may be the worst perpetrators. I've actually heard instructors tell their students to just ape the instructor's upper body movements and the feet "will just follow." Wrong. To throw an educated punch, you need to have educated feet. True, some boxers have a natural aptitude for footwork, but you *can* train to develop and improve it. That many do not is insanity.

This is one subject that made all three of our Angry Young Men—Dempsey, Driscoll, and Nadi—well, so angry. They all expressed dissatisfaction with the lack of high-quality instruction regarding footwork. "[All the real champions]," Driscoll observed, "are men who hit straight, use the left hand as it should be used, are fully aware of the fact the feet are as important as the hands in the boxing game."[5]

Of footwork, Nadi complained, "Of all the teachers I have seen at work I have yet to see one train his pupils in this essential work. They simply let them find out for themselves. In the best cases this means a tremendous loss of time before the pupil familiarizes himself with combat tactics."[6]

Recall the ways in which Dempsey declared boxing was "being taught wrong nearly everywhere." Four of those reasons involve footwork:

- Beginners are not grounded in the four principal methods of putting body weight in fast motion: (a) falling step, (b) leg spring, (c) shoulder whirl, (d) upward surge.

- Explosive straight punching has become almost a lost art because instructors place so much emphasis on shoulder whirl, that beginners are taught wrongfully to punch straight without stepping whenever possible.

- Failure to teach the falling step ("trigger step") for straight punching has resulted in the left jab being used generally as a light, auxiliary weapon for making openings and "setting up," instead of as a stunning blow.

- Beginners are not warned that taking long steps with hooks may open up those hooks into swings.[7]

NOT JUST COVERING DISTANCE

A common misconception is that footwork is only about getting from Point A to Point B. Many instructors gloss over footwork, thinking it beneath them to master the fundamentals. They figure all the action takes place from the torso up. So, they gallop into battle and then wonder why their punches are so powderpuff.

Dempsey knew footwork was the answer. The falling step, leg spring, shoulder whirl—yes, even shoulder whirl—and upward surge to which he referred are all aspects of footwork. What people often do not realize is that footwork is so much more than just covering distance. Punch mechanics are determined by alignment, and alignment starts from the ground. How you position your feet determines the alignment of your legs. Your legs are attached to and determine the position of your trunk. And your arms are attached to your trunk. For some punches, like the hook and the uppercut, the arm is really just along for the ride. It's the body that does all the work, because that's where all your weight is. If you want to avoid being an arm puncher, you need to throw your weight into your punches. And to do that, you need footwork.

The same is true of defensive moves. To remain in balance for stability and mobility, you cannot rely on moving only from the waist up. You must correctly position your center of gravity, and to do that while in motion, you need footwork.

A lot of essential footwork is almost imperceptible to the untrained eye. When you shift your weight from one leg to another—as in a hook punch or bobbing and weaving—that's footwork. Keeping your left heel off the ground, not too high and not too low, that's precise footwork. When making tiny adjustments—a matter of inches—while maintaining the fighting measure, that's footwork. If you watch the footage of Bruce demonstrating the straight lead at the International Karate Tournament in 1967,[8] you'll see him throwing that punch from a seemingly stationary position. True, he may not be covering any distance, but there's a lot of footwork going on there. There's the push-off and a tremendous transfer of weight from the left leg to the lead right leg.

People have been baffled by Bruce's legendary 1-inch punch and what Hayward Nishioka referred to as a puzzling "twitch" of the hips. What they may not realize is that there's a heck of a lot of push-off coming from the rear leg and a transfer in energy to the lead leg that makes that hip twitch possible. You may have to look carefully to even notice that he is coming off the ground at all, but it's there. That's the push-off in place, and it makes all the difference. As you'll find in his notes, Bruce did not describe footwork only in terms of covering distance. "Foot work can add weight and power to a punch or a kick," he wrote.[9] This is because footwork contributes to force production by determining your weight distribution. Footwork in JKD serves as much more than a mere transport system. It's the key to alignment and leverage.

Speaking of hips, we talk a lot about using the hip as a guide to our mechanics. We always want to move in a way so that the hip will be pointing toward the target, whether that be punching or kicking mechanics. Always remember, though, you cannot get your hips in the proper position without first moving your feet. This is what Dempsey was getting at. The falling step, leg spring, and upward surge may not involve covering any distance, but they are all important elements of footwork. And the shoulder whirl to which he refers is impossible without footwork. To move your shoulders, you must move your trunk. To move your trunk, you need to move your legs. And to move your legs, you need to move your feet. All punches really do start from the ground up.

THE FIGHTING MEASURE

It goes without saying that in order to successfully land a blow, you must first move toward your opponent. A forceful punch means little if you are not in position to throw it. Of course, if you're close enough to land a blow, then you're also close enough to get tagged yourself. This is why maintenance of the *fighting measure* is so important. According to Crosnier, the fighting measure is the distance at which a fencer cannot hit or be hit without a full lunge. One of the main purposes of playing with distance is to make your opponent misjudge that fighting measure by luring or tricking him into your striking distance.[10]

The fighting measure—or judgment of distance—is crucial. Without it, you won't be able to reach your target. Even worse, you can expect to take a lot of shots. And how do you maintain the fighting measure? Footwork. See Figure 73.

Figure 73: *Footwork makes maintaining the fighting measure possible.*

It's worth noting here that Crosnier was a stickler for good form and the fundamentals of the on-guard position. Without good form, good footwork is impossible to achieve. The following passage was underlined in Bruce Lee's copy of Crosnier's *Fencing with the Foil*:

> The fencer practicing his footwork will find that his mobility will be greatly handicapped if his on-guard position is not perfect. An incorrect distribution of weight will mean that he will have to shift his body forward, or backward, in order to be able to free the leg that is carrying the extra burden when he wishes to move it. He will readily appreciate, then, the necessity of paying attention to his basic stance and position on guard.[11]

We'll come back to the fighting measure when we discuss how to apply the straight lead. For now, though, know that maintenance of the fighting measure is where you are safe and that it is achieved through footwork, footwork, footwork.

THE LEFT FOOT DICTATES DISTANCE

Before we get into the mechanics of footwork as it relates to the straight lead, realize that it is the left foot that is your distance regulator. The push-off from your left foot is what enables you to reach an opponent—not your upper body or arm reach. A common mistake is overreaching with the right hand and upper body. In this case, your center of gravity—as discussed earlier—will overtake your front leg, taking you out of your base of support and thereby unbalancing you. This will put you in a precarious position to ward off counterattacks, will hamper your recovery to the stance, and compromise your punching force.[12]

To reach your target, then, you must use your feet. The movement from your upper body should be consistent. You will rotate at the hips, slightly lean forward, and extend your right arm to the same degree *every* time you throw that straight lead. What changes then? The distance you cover with your feet—more specifically, the distance you cover with the push-off.

You can practice this by varying the distance you cover with the push-off. Sometimes as you can see from the footage of Bruce's 1-inch punch, you will push off in place and not cover any distance. Other times, you will need to push off from long range to reach your target. Be careful, though. Do not increase the distance you cover with the push-off until you have achieved sufficient control at a shorter distance. Precision and control should be your chief objectives. I'll talk about how to achieve this shortly.

TYPES OF FOOTWORK

At its most basic level, footwork involves moving in only four directions—forward, backward, left, and right. Maybe that doesn't sound too exciting, but the variations of how you move in those four directions, the physics and precision involved, make those four directions infinitely complex. There's sidestepping left and right. There's also pivoting left and right. There's pivoting on the bounce, the half-beat, or with a bob and weave. You can step and slide backward, push step backward, or pendulum step backward. You can pendulum step while coming out of a pivoting bounce! The combinations are endless.

And then there's the step that seems to give guys fits in Ted Wong's seminars—the "fancy step," as he calls it, which is something of a cross between a sideways jumping jack and a sidestep. You'll see Oscar De La Hoya and a number of other boxers use this one whenever they need to change directions quickly.

Now imagine being able to fire off a straight lead—or a variation of a straight—off of any of these steps no matter where your weight is distributed. Most arts require you to "complete" a step before you are in position to fire a shot. You step with one foot and then must land with the other. And *then* you can throw a punch. If you've studied music or dance at all, you can think of this as one whole beat. The step with the front foot is the first beat. Landing of the back foot is the "and" of that beat. Then you're ready to step again. That's the second beat. Landing with the rear foot is the "and" of the second beat.

Most arts only allow for punching "*on* the beat." With good footwork, though, you can punch on the "and"—or the *half-beat*.[13] This is what makes for educated feet. Since most arts don't train to incorporate the half-beat, this gives you a definite tactical advantage. While your opponent's still settling into position, setting up for the next beat, you've already popped him on the half-beat. Working with half-beats exponentially expands your options. Playing with distance and time makes you unpredictable, keeps your opponent guessing. You can set him up by creating patterns and then breaking them—trick him into coming within your striking distance. All of this is accomplished through footwork.

And in JKD, your straight is the main weapon with which you'll be setting up your attacks. To be able to use those half-beats, then, you'll need to be able to throw that lead punch from anywhere. The window of striking opportunity closes in a matter of milliseconds. Good footwork allows you to take advantage of those opportunities. You can throw a lead from the on-guard position, while your front foot is still in the air, with your weight distributed mostly in your front foot, or before your rear foot has landed. Without footwork, none of this is possible.

To include a comprehensive guide to footwork is beyond the scope of this book. What I'll cover here will only illustrate the ways of advancing forward with the straight lead. But keep in mind this is only a tiny glimpse of what educated footwork is all about.

THE STEP AND SLIDE

The step and slide is the most basic and most frequently used footwork step. It's not used to launch an offensive, but it's crucial as a distance regulator.[14, 15, 16] The step and slide is how we maintain the fighting measure and play with it in order to create setups. I call it "stalking footwork."

To execute the step and slide, as always, you'll start from the on-guard position. Your weight should be distributed evenly between both feet. Lift your right foot and step no more than 6 inches forward. Your weight should still be about 50-50, even as your right foot is above the ground. Just let gravity do its thing and gently land heel first. As your right heel is landing your left leg should be sliding forward the same distance that your right foot advanced. It should land just after the front foot does. You can spot examples of Bruce Lee's step and slide in *Return of the Dragon* scenes with Chuck Norris. You'll see him using it as a distance regulator as he's judging when to intercept Chuck's attacks.

A note about the word "slide"—this does not mean your foot drags along the ground. Your left foot should just glide up the same distance that your right foot moved. In both cases, you lift your feet just enough to clear the ground. Remember footwork must be economical.

When practicing the step and slide your main objective should be precision. You want to be in the stance at all times. If your right foot moves 2 inches forward, your left should follow by 2 inches. In the beginning, check your stance after every step. Are you aligned properly? Did your stance end exactly the way you started? If not, make the required adjustments and take the time to get the feel of the correct stance. Try again. With practice, you will soon land in the on-guard position without having to make any adjustments. See Figures 74 and 75.

Figure 74: The step and slide from the on-guard position.

Figure 75: *Whatever distance the right foot advances, the left foot must follow up an equal distance so that the integrity of the stance is maintained.*

THE PUSH STEP

The push step is a quicker way of advancing than the step and slide. The step and slide is a two-step process. First you step, and then you slide. The step is initiated with the front foot.

The push step, on the other hand, is initiated with the left foot. You are pushing off the ground with the ball of your left foot. Compared to the step and slide, there is much less time between the landing of the right heel and the ball of your left foot. You generate more force with the push step, and, therefore, it is the push step—not the step and slide—that is used for quicker advances and evasions.[17]

As is always the case with footwork, precision is priority. Every time you push step, you should finish in the stance—just as you started. It's important to remember that even though the push step is explosive, it needs to be controlled. It's a quiet motion that requires a clean landing. My students have all kinds of descriptions for the push-off. Everything from bunny hops to cricket jumps to ninja-like, but my all-time favorite description is that of a rat pissing on lint cotton! A bit graphic, but you have to admit that's gotta be pretty quiet.

PUSH-OFF VERSUS PUSH STEP

We've discussed the push-off in detail in Chapter Four. I'd just like to draw a bit of a distinction between the push step and the push-off. The push-off might be considered the push step taken to the next degree. This is where you'll generate the explosiveness needed to launch punches. Think of the difference in intensity between a feeler jab and a stiff one. You would probably use the push step for the feeler and the push-off to fire a stiff jab.

I can't overemphasize this notion of explosiveness. I've already referenced Nadi and Bruce's descriptions of the left foot: piston, cobra, spark plug, engine, and my favorite—"one of the mightiest springs in all creation." There's good reason for such vivid and seemingly dramatic descriptions. The intensity and power of explosive punching originate from the push-off.

THE PIVOT STEP

Obviously, in a fight you do not move only along a linear plane. You don't just move forward and backward as fencers do along the strip. The pivot step allows you to move at an angle and is often very useful for delivering blows while moving out of harm's way.[18]

To pivot right, lift your right foot just enough to clear the ground. Use your right toe as a rough pointer. Once you are aligned with the target, let your right foot rest on the ground. Then bring your left foot around so that you are back in the on-guard position.

Likewise, to pivot left, lift your left foot first. Swing your left leg around and let your body turn with it. When you're aligned with the target, let your left foot rest on the ground. Pick up your right foot and angle it until you are in the correct position.

Again, you always, always, always want to maintain the integrity of the stance. What you are essentially doing is taking the stance and merely changing your angle so that you can move with a moving opponent and keep him within striking distance. Remember the gunsight? You always want to move to keep your opponent within the gunsight. See Figures 76 and 77.

Figure 76: *Pivot step starting from the on-guard position.*

Figure 77: *To whatever degree your front foot pivots, the back foot must swing around enough so that you are aligned with the target in the proper stance.*

The pivot step can be tricky in the beginning. There is a certain amount of anticipation, distance, and muscle memory that must go into pivoting without having to make adjustments. In the beginning, you will most likely have to make minor adjustments. Just know that this is natural and that precision will come with enough time and practice.

Also remember that the direction in which you pivot is always the foot that comes off the ground first. So, if you want to pivot to the right (counterclockwise), you'll pick up your right foot first. Then the left (rear) foot swings around so that you adjust back into the stance.

If you are pivoting left (clockwise), pick up your left (rear) foot first, swing your left leg around, and adjust back into the stance by pivoting your right (front) foot. Always remember that when you pivot you want to wind up in the stance with your opponent within your gunsight. Remember our imaginary line from the stance chapter? You always want that line that runs from your right toe and under your left arch to be in line with the target.

You'll see quite a bit of pivoting in *Return of the Dragon* as Bruce moves around Chuck Norris, evading, ducking, and countering. You'll notice that pivoting allows him to get out of the way while staying close enough to deliver an offensive. You'll also see some of the variations of pivoting. As I've just mentioned, you can add upper body moves, such as ducking and weaving, to the pivot step. But there are also countless footwork combinations involving pivot stepping. By combining pivoting with half-beat footwork, you give yourself more angles and timing options than many other arts do.

Advanced Footwork

The push-off is the starting point for throwing the straight lead, but in the heat of battle, you don't always have the luxury of setting up in the stance in its purest form. Maybe you're in the middle of a step and slide when a striking opportunity opens up. Or you might be moving backward. In such cases, how do you manage to fire off a straight lead? As is usually the case, footwork is the answer.

Again, we just can't adequately cover the topic of footwork here, but I will touch on a few steps to give you a sneak preview of how the straight lead works while you are in motion. In an actual fighting or sparring situation, the dimension of your footwork changes so drastically that the most basic steps—the step and slide, the push step, and the pivot—actually take a back seat. *They* become the supplemental footwork, and the more advanced steps—bouncing, half-beats, and the steps we'll discuss shortly—take center stage. There's just no time in a real fight for whole-beat footwork, so the basic steps become almost unrecognizable as they are linked to and blended with more advanced footwork.

Weight up Front

When you step and slide, even though you strive to distribute your weight 50-50, there is a very brief moment when your weight is slightly shifted to your front foot, while your other foot is in the air on its way to touching the ground. You need to be able to fire off a shot at the instant an opportunity presents itself.

In such cases, you will merely *touch* the ground with your right foot. This is different from a regular landing when you actually let that weight settle into the ground before allowing the left foot to land. No, you want to get a shot off as your right foot is on the ground. You can, but you must not allow yourself to put your weight into that front foot. Lightly touch the ground—just enough for balance—with your front foot so that your rear foot can land, and then immediately push off for an attack.

Pendulum Step

The pendulum step is a great defensive counter. As your opponent advances, you can deliver a straight lead without jamming yourself, allowing you to maintain leverage. The pendulum is often used to avoid kicks, but it's good for warding off attacks in general.[19] To execute this step from the stance, you'll swing your lead leg backward as your rear leg swings in the same direction. You will place your right foot where your left foot was. Sometimes we refer to this as a "replacement" step. See Figures 78 and 79.

You'll see Bruce pendulum step all the time in his films—at the beginning of *Enter the Dragon* with Sammo Hung, in battle with Chuck Norris, and in *The Game of Death* fight sequences.

Figure 78: *Pendulum step from on-guard position.*

Figure 79: *Swing your front leg back and let gravity do the work. You can use this step to evade kicks or throw defensive jabs.*

STEALING STEP

Sometimes you need a little extra oomph to bridge the gap to your opponent. You can give yourself a little extra push with what we call the stealing step. Your left foot will slide forward—quickly—no more than 3 or 4 inches and then you take off. This lessens the distance between your left and right foot and gives you a little extra leverage from which to push off. The very movement of the left foot also gives you a little extra momentum. It's a *very* fast, subtle movement—think hair trigger. It's also not something you would use from a stationary stance because that little extra movement telegraphs your punch. But if you are already in motion or in hot pursuit, the stealing step can get you a little more explosiveness and distance and makes for a much more penetrating attack. See Figures 80 through 82.

A PEEK AT OTHER VARIATIONS

We've only covered a few ways to launch a straight lead moving either forward or in reverse. Just know that there are so many other ways to use footwork and the lead hand. You can sidestep, curve, and pivot, allowing you to angle your punches. You can use what we call the "fancy step" to change directions quickly and with little effort while throwing out a straight. These steps are all linked with bouncing and half-beat steps. The skip step gives you an option to hit should you be caught with *all* of your weight in the front foot. The stutter step is a way to play with momentum and timing.

And speaking of timing, there are all sorts of ways to create, break, and syncopate rhythm to confuse your opponent. This is accomplished through footwork.

SMALL STEPS

There's an entire section in *Commentaries on the Martial Way* that is devoted to footwork and throughout it you will find Bruce's emphasis on small steps.

First, small steps are easier to control. A lot of people think if they cover more distance with one step, they are being efficient. The problem with this, though, is that the longer your stride, the more time you spend in a vulnerable, off-balance position. The larger the step, the more you deviate from the on-guard position. This will take your center of gravity outside the foundation base, setting you off-balance. You will also create more momentum, making it difficult to stop on a dime, and nearly impossible to reverse directions.

In addition to lack of control, larger movements take you further out of position for follow ups or counterstrikes. It costs you precious time when you deviate unnecessarily from the stance.

Figure 80: *Stealing step from the on-guard position.*

Figure 81: *The back foot advances no more than a few inches giving you extra leverage. From there, you launch into the push-off . . .*

Figure 82: *. . . and land back in the stance.*

Small steps contribute to efficiency. It's better to take several controlled small steps than one big stride. Suppose that you have to change directions. You can do so with small steps. But if you're in the middle of that big step, you'll have to wait longer to complete it so you can take another one.

One final note about small steps—it doesn't mean aimless bouncing. Some people mistake footwork for purposeless movement. If your opponent is jitterbugging in front of you at a safe distance, fine, let him wear himself out. You don't have to join him. Relax. You bounce only when you need to—when your opponent's about to close in, when you need to regain some balance or change direction quickly. But you just don't bounce in place for the sake of bouncing.

Remember economy is one of the JKD roots:

"Economical footwork is the soundest kind, and the Jeet Kune Do man's aim should always be to move as little as possible." [20]

Supplemental Training

One of the most useful tools for getting light on your feet is the jump rope. Skipping not only develops the endurance you need—especially in those arches—but it is also a great training tool for body control. Nothing gets you light on your feet faster than skipping. You'll learn how to negotiate your body weight in motion, while developing muscular and cardiovascular endurance.[21, 22]

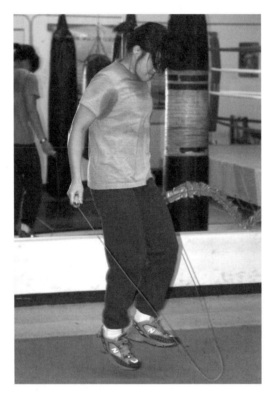

Figure 83: *Skipping rope is one of the best ways to supplement your footwork training.*

NO SUBSTITUTE FOR THE REAL THING

Of course, there is no other way to get good at something than by doing the actual thing. All the running and leg presses in the world aren't going to result in good footwork, because you need to do the neuromuscular programming. There's just no way around this. You have to practice footwork.

And once you feel pretty comfortable on your feet, the next step is to add the upper body into the equation by shadowboxing. Ted Wong stresses that this is the best thing you can do for your footwork[23] because it's closer to what you'd actually be doing in a fight. If you throw out a straight lead, you'll need to properly recover before you can shoot out another. You also need to learn the footwork that's going to allow you to fire a straight lead coming out of a shoulder roll, bob, or weave. And if you're chasing an opponent, you need to know how footwork will enable you to bridge the gap. Shadowboxing makes all of this possible.

This is where your body gets to experiment. You'll learn how to best adjust your body weight while in motion. I've already talked about body feel in the discussion of the stance. Shadowboxing is where you acquire body feel in motion. Have fun with it. Acquiring new skills should be an enjoyable process, especially when you start to feel balanced and in control of your body. There is a certain satisfaction and power you should derive from that kind of control.

Figure 84: *Even when hitting the bag, footwork should be your first priority.*

PRECISION

When practicing footwork, precision is the name of the game. Always aim to maintain the integrity of the stance. If you step forward 3 inches with the right foot, make sure your left foot slides up 3 inches. In the beginning, every time you take a step, stop. Check your alignment. Is that imaginary line that touches your right toe passing under the arch of your left foot? If not, you need to correct the position of your feet.

This may sound a bit obsessive-compulsive, but remember that when learning new techniques, all sorts of neuromuscular connections are being made. If your practice is sloppy, you will be programming incorrectly. And unlearning and correcting bad habits is more difficult and time-consuming than learning a technique right the first time around.

Footwork is anything but boring. This is where you cultivate body feel. This is where it all starts—where you learn to shift your weight so that you feel comfortable and balanced in motion. As I've discussed, punches are generated from the ground up. Alignment starts with the feet. You cannot expect to generate forceful punches with sloppy footwork. Before you can move on to punching, speed and more advanced footwork, you need to start with the basics.

Check yourself in the mirror, draw lines with chalk, use the patterns on your kitchen linoleum—whatever you can in the name of precision. What we are trying to do is program those neuromuscular pathways so that it will become second nature. Soon your body will *know* when it's in correct alignment. And after that, it will know how to get there with fewer and fewer adjustments until no more adjustments are needed. That's the kind of efficiency you should strive for. This isn't just for beginners either. You can never be too precise.

A matter of an inch or two may not seem like much, but remember how much of a difference it made in our experiment with the stance. Your alignment may not be spot on in combat, but the closer you are, the better you'll be. You'll have that much more advantage over your opponent. You may think I'm splitting hairs here, that footwork is boring, and that I'm a bit obsessive compulsive about precision, so I'd like to take a moment to close this chapter with a few words from basketball great, Coach John Wooden:

> These seemingly trivial matters, taken together and added to many, many other so-called trivial matters build into something very big: namely, your success.
>
> You will find that success and attention to details, the smallest details, usually go hand in hand, in basketball and elsewhere in your life.
>
> When you see a successful individual, a champion, a "winner," you can be very sure that you are looking at an individual who pays great attention to the perfection of minor details.[24]

I can assure you that Bruce Lee paid attention to those details, and I'm sure he was never bored when practicing footwork. And while you and I may not be Bruce Lee, we get a little closer to being the best we can be by paying attention to the finer points in all areas of our lives.

NOTES

[1] Bruce Lee, ed. John Little, *Jeet Kune Do: Bruce Lee's Commentaries on the Martial Way* (Boston: Tuttle Publishing, 1997), p. 199.

[2] Aldo Nadi, *On Fencing*, (Bangor, ME: Laureate Press, 1994), p. 63.

[3] Vijay Prashad, "Summer of Bruce" in *Screaming Monkeys* (Minneapolis, MN: Coffee House Press), p. 256. Prashad writes,

In an instance of classic cross-fertilization, the great boxer Sugar Ray Leonard told an interviewer in 1982 that "one of the guys who influenced me wasn't a boxer. I always loved the catlike reflexes and the artistry of Bruce Lee and I wanted to do in boxing what he was able to do in karate [sic]. I started watching his movies before he became really popular in *Enter the Dragon* and I patterned myself after a lot of his ways."

[4] Lee, ed. John Little, *Jeet Kune Do: Bruce Lee's Commentaries on the Martial Way*, p. 193.

[5] Jim Driscoll, *The Straight Left and How To Cultivate It* (London: Athletic Publications, LTD.), p. 13.

[6] Nadi, *On Fencing*, p. 156.

[7] Jack Dempsey, *Championship Fighting: Explosive Punching and Aggressive Defence* (New York: Prentice Hall, Inc., 1950), p. 18.

[8] See *Bruce Lee: A Warrior's Journey*, at 29 min, 35 sec.

[9] Lee, ed. John Little, *Jeet Kune Do: Bruce Lee's Commentaries on the Martial Way*, p. 201.

[10] Bruce Lee, *Tao of Jeet Kune Do* (Santa Clarita, CA, Ohara Publications, Inc., 1975), p. 139. Compare Bruce's definition of the "fighting measure" to the "fencing measure" in Roger Crosnier, *Fencing with the Foil: Instruction and Technique* (London: Faber and Faber, 1948), pp. 38–39: "The *fencing measure* is the distance which a fencer keeps in relationship to his opponent. It is such that he cannot be hit unless his opponent lunges fully at him."

[11] Ibid., p. 40.

[12] Ibid., p. 56. Compare with Lee, ed. John Little, *Jeet Kune Do: Bruce Lee's Commentaries on the Martial Way*, p. 189: "The pupil must never be permitted to lean forward in attempting to reach the target. The master must regulate his distance in such a manner that his pupil does not have to shift his weight and so lose his balance."

[13] Nadi, *On Fencing*, p. 183.

[14] Ted Wong with John Little, "The Key to Defeating Any Attack: The Footwork of Jun Fan Jeet Kune Do," *Bruce Lee: The Official Publication & Voice of the Jun Fan Jeet Kune Do Nucleus*, December, 1998, p. 81.

[15] Bruce Lee and M. Uyehara, *Bruce Lee's Fighting Method* (Burbank, CA: Ohara Publications, Inc., 1978), pp. 42–43.

[16] See William Cheung and Ted Wong, *Wing Chun Kung Fu/ Jeet Kune Do: A Comparison Vol. 1* (Santa Clarita, CA: Ohara Publications, Inc., 1990), pp. 30-31, for Ted Wong's explanation of the step and slide, also known as the advance shuffle.

[17] Ted Wong with John Little, "The Key to Defeating Any Attack: The Footwork of Jun Fan Jeet Kune Do," *Bruce Lee: The Official Publication & Voice of the Jun Fan Jeet Kune Do Nucleus*, December, 1998, pp. 81.

[18] Dempsey, *Championship Fighting: Explosive Punching and Aggressive Defence*, pp. 97–98.

[19] Cheung and Wong, *Wing Chun Kung Fu/Jeet Kune Do: A Comparison Vol. 1*, pp. 36–37. For Ted Wong's explanation of the pendulum step.

[20] Lee, ed. John Little, *Jeet Kune Do: Bruce Lee's Commentaries on the Martial Way*, pp. 195–199.

[21] Ibid., p. 195. Bruce was a big proponent of skipping rope. "Skipping rope is a wonderful exercise to learn how to handle one's body agilely," he wrote. "It is a good footwork supplementary exercise."

[22] For more on skipping rope, see Lee and Uyehara, *Bruce Lee's Fighting Method*, p. 10.

[23] Wong, "The Key to Defeating Any Attack: The Footwork of Jun Fan Jeet Kune Do," December, 1998, p. 84.

[24] John Wooden with Steve Jamison, *Wooden: A Lifetime of Observations and Reflections on and off the Court* (Chicago: Contemporary Books, 1997), pp. 60–63. Perhaps the greatest basketball coach of all time, John Wooden was a stickler for details, right down to the precise sizing and lacing of his players' shoes. His famous sock-fitting protocol is the stuff of basketball legend:

> I believe in the basics. Attention to, and perfection of, tiny details that might commonly be overlooked. They may seem trivial, perhaps even laughable to those who don't understand, but they aren't. They are fundamental to your progress in basketball, business, and life. They are the difference between champions and near champions.

WHY THE STRAIGHT LEAD?

W e've discussed the how-to's of the straight lead, and you should now have a basic understanding of its structure and sound roots in the sciences of biomechanics and physics. Now it's time to address the whys of the straight lead and delve a little into fighting science. In this chapter, there'll be a bit of overlap with the earlier discussion of mechanics and with the next chapter, which deals with application.

In his copy of Edwin Haislet's *Boxing*, Bruce Lee outlined some of the advantages of the straight lead:

1. Faster—the shortest distance between two points is a straight line

2. More accurate—less chance of missing and is surer than other punches

3. Greater Frequency of Hits—more damage can be done

4. Balance is less disturbed—safer

5. Safer, surer, and easier

6. Less injurious to one's hand[1, 2, 3]

FASTER

Let's start with the first item on Bruce's list. The straight lead is the fastest possible punch for several reasons, the first of which is a simple matter of geometry—the shortest distance between two points is a straight line. A straight punch will always beat a curving, hooking, or swinging punch.

You'll find reminders of this basic fact repeated over and over from JKD's major boxing influences—Dempsey, Driscoll, and Haislet.[4] As Driscoll dryly stated:

> There is surely no need to refer to Euclid for confirmation of the obvious fact that the shortest distance between any two points must of necessity be the straight line between them. Every boxer, no matter how small his intelligence otherwise, must at once admit as much—with, of course, the natural sequel that a straight punch must always get home before a round arm swinging one, provided, of course, that both start at the same time.[5]

To this I'd like to add that a skilled executor of the straight may even land a shot before a swinging punch even if it is initiated *after* the swing, provided that timing, accuracy, and sound mechanics are all in place. See Figure 85.

Figure 85: *The straight always wins. Here, Ted Wong's corkscrew hook (a variation of the straight lead) will land long before my hook will.*

Dempsey made a similar argument also noting that a straight punch from either the front or rear hand would beat a punch with an arc.[6, 7] The straight-line argument may be common sense, and in Dempsey's day, this was considered common knowledge, but it seems to have been forgotten among today's less educated punchers.

It isn't just the straight line that makes the lead punch fast. When you align yourself properly in the stance, your lead hand is closer to the target. As Bruce observed, "It is a potent offensive and defensive weapon because of its advanced position—it is halfway to the target before starting."[8]

And while Dempsey's orthodox stance was set up with the strong (right) hand in the back, he stressed the more important role that the lead hand plays, mainly because of its proximity to the target.[9] The combined effect of hitting in a straight line and with the hand that is in an advanced position not only enables you to throw the lead punch faster—it takes less effort to do so. So while we're on the subject of economy of motion, let's skip to item number four on our list of straight lead advantages.

BALANCE IS LESS DISTURBED

We've already established the solidity of the JKD stance. We've discussed Newton's law of action and reaction, and we've talked about the importance of balance and center of gravity and how to maintain balance while in motion. Looking at the bigger picture, though, it's important to realize that the stance is actually set up for the straight lead. The JKD on-guard position is constructed so that we can throw the straight lead with the least deviation from the stance.

Because the lead hand has less distance to travel to the target, the straight lead gives us the advantage of "economy of time and balance."[10, 11, 12] A shorter distance to the target means less deviation from the stance, less recovery time, and faster follow-up punches. And, of course, less disruption of balance means better mobility, successful evasion and counters, and the ability to get off more shots.

As Driscoll noted, "If one misses with a huge swing, or "haymaker," as the Americans term it, one is practically certain to become unbalanced, and consequently at the mercy of one's opponent."[13] I suggest you try this out with a little focus mitt drill. The mitt holder should occasionally cause the puncher to miss straight leads and hooks. Even if you are throwing your straight leads and hooks correctly, you should notice that it takes much more effort to recover from a missed hook.

NONTELEGRAPHIC

It's not on Bruce's list, but economical properties of the straight lead give us an obvious corollary: the straight lead is the least telegraphic punch in the JKD arsenal. Less distance means less effort, less deviation from the stance, and less time. Less time means less warning. Your opponent literally will never know what hit him.

Both Dempsey and Bruce had a lot to say about being nontelegraphic.[14, 15] Driscoll wrote that not only is a swinging punch slower to reach a target, it's virtually one big telegraph.[16] Even if a fighter's most forceful punch is a swinging one, what good is it if his opponent can see it coming a mile away? That leaves your opponent plenty of time to get out of the way, or worse, send a deadly counter.

It's not just that the swinging punch must travel a greater distance than the straight. The angle from which the straight originates makes it very difficult to detect. Think about it. A swinging punch must traverse from left to right or vice versa across your field of vision. Similarly, with an uppercut, you'll see an arm and a fist move vertically. All you see when facing a straight lead, though, is a fist from a certain distance—and then a fist in your face!

See Figures 86 through 89.

Figure 86: *The straight gives no warning. First there's a fist at a distance . . .*

Figure 87: . . . then there's a fist in your face.

Figure 88: In contrast to straight punching, Hook punching
reveals much more across your field of vision.

Figure 89: *You will actually see your opponent's fist move left or right, giving you more time to evade or counter.*

ACCURACY

Getting back to Bruce's list, the straight lead gives us more control and accuracy than other punches. All the issues of balance, recovery, telegraphing, and distance contribute to greater accuracy of the straight lead. The straight also allows for full extension of the arm.[17]As I've already noted, the relative slowness of arcing punches gives your opponent time to recognize the punch and get out of the way, and if your opponent is moving away, the shorter reach afforded by a hook or swing makes a successful landing less likely.[18]

It's helpful here to remember the analogous evolution of sword fighting and the eventual preference of the rapier over the broadsword. Accurate thrusting through the small vulnerable spots between plates of metal armor proved much more effective than trying to slash through armor.[19] Driscoll argued that the evolution of the straight lead had followed in the footsteps of the rapier:

> The "Bear-Cat" brigade are bludgeon fighters, who disdain the use of the rapier, for the simple reason that they are utterly ignorant of the finer points of the game. Yet the whole history of single combat refutes their argument. Man did not abandon the club as a weapon because he preferred the rapier as a parlour

pastime, but because the sword proved itself to be the more useful weapon. And it was a similar process of discovery that the axe, which had superseded the club, gave way to the sword and the buckler, then to the case swords, until even the broadsword and sabre were abandoned in favour of the rapier.[20]

Driscoll argued that uneducated spectators were attracted to the drama of the swinging punch and the broad strokes of the saber. The same could be said of today's bloody brawlers and staged film fights. Swings are easy for people to see. They look good for the camera. But in a competitive or more realistic situation, you don't want your opponent to see you! You don't want him to know what hit him.

Getting back to the subject of accuracy, a swinging punch is much harder to control, and therefore, much harder to aim accurately. When you throw a hook, it's very hard to change directions. Once you've committed to moving, say, left or right, that's it. Also remember how difficult it is to recover to the on-guard position from a swinging punch. But the compactness of the straight lead and its straight-as-an-arrow trajectory make it easier to change directions, even in mid-punch. By using footwork, you can make minor adjustments and still hit a fast-moving target.

And while a straight lead may have slightly less force than a haymaker, what good is having a haymaker if you can never land one? Of course, missing a haymaker leaves you in a very vulnerable position for counters. A perfect, stiff, straight lead, on the other hand, delivers more than enough force to get the job done, and it can do so more often (see Figure 90). Which leads to the next item on the list. . . .

GREATER FREQUENCY OF HITS

Building on what I've already discussed, a faster, nontelegraphic, more accurate, and closer-to-the-target punch means that you're going to be able to land more often, and as Bruce wrote, "more damage can be done."[21] Also, the efficiency involved in delivering the punch contributes to faster recovery, so you can fire more shots. The efficiency doesn't only occur in terms of time and motion. With more controlled recovery and minimized deviation from the stance, coupled with proper mechanics, you'll become fatigued less easily. You could throw straight leads all day.

Greater frequency of hits gets your opponent off balance, puts him on the defensive, and creates more opportunities for you to finish him off.[22] Of course, a properly thrown single straight lead can pack more than enough wallop on its own to finish an opponent.

Figure 90: *Working on the focus mitts is one of the best ways to develop accuracy.*

LESS INJURIOUS TO ONE'S HANDS

I've covered this already in the chapter on mechanics. Remember the experiment with Dempsey's power line and how much more stable your wrist was when you made contact with the bottom three knuckles instead of the top two. Again, this is a simple matter of human anatomy. Straight hitting with the thumb up allows you to take advantage of the power line that runs from your shoulder through your arm to those bottom three knuckles.[23] You'll not only hit with more force but also prevent hand injuries by keeping the wrong knuckles from bearing excessive force on impact.[24]

Driscoll added that swingers could expect shorter fighting careers because they put their hands at unnecessary risk. He argued that the accuracy of the straight punch increased the frequency of landing with the bottom three knuckles, putting the boxer in the best position to distribute the absorption of impact. The swinging punch, on the other hand, has a less likely chance of landing squarely, putting the hand at greater risk.

It follows, then, that the straight punch plays a large part in contributing to a fighter's longevity. "The swinger's hands or wrists," Dempsey wrote, "*must* go in time, and in short time at that."[25]

S A F E R ,   S U R E R ,   E A S I E R

Going down Bruce's checklist so far, we've discussed how the straight is surer in accuracy, easier in terms of mechanics, distance, recovery, and balance, and safer in its structure, which protects the striking hand.

Let's take this safety issue one step further, though, and talk about how all the straight lead advantages thus far contribute to what Dempsey called "aggressive defence."

" P U N C H   R A N K S   F I R S T "

In these times of big-money sports and pay-per-view bloodbath extravaganzas, it's hard to believe that there was a time when boxing was considered the "Useful Science of Defence."[26] That the original purpose of boxing had been forgotten was what compelled both Driscoll and Dempsey to write *The Straight Left and How to Cultivate It* and *Championship Fighting: Explosive Punching and Aggressive Defence*, respectively. It's no coincidence that Dempsey included the words "aggressive defence" in the title, for its neglect is something that infuriated him.[27]

At present, it seems things haven't changed for the better, but at least it's comforting to know that Driscoll complained of the same things in the 1920s, blaming "decadence in boxing" on the lost art of defense. Driscoll wrote that offense and defense are inextricably linked but that the latter had been forgotten:

> Boxing is, after all, the art of self-defence first, last, and all the time, and that success is only to be won by remembering that defence is not only the chief thing to be considered, but that attack can only be allowed to come into the picture at all when it is employed as an auxiliary to defence, and in the old sense that the strongest form of defence is a vigorous attack, carried out mainly and almost entirely with a view to the minimizing of the risk, or the repulse of all counter attack.[28]

Similarly, Dempsey so believed in the straight punch as a means of defense that he structured his book around it, choosing to painstakingly describe the mechanics of punching before ever describing a single defensive move. He then introduced the section on defense with a chapter entitled "Punch Ranks First" to explain that the straight punch is the first line of defense.

"The best defence in fighting is an aggressive defence," he wrote. "Each defensive move must be *accompanied by a counterpunch* or be *followed immediately* by a *counterpunch*. And you cannot counter properly if you do not know how to punch." He went on to explain how "fellows" who have no confidence in their punching abilities develop "defence complexes," resulting in unnecessary footwork, back pedaling, pulled punches, and an overall bad time of it in the ring.[29]

And all that running around is tiring! It's much more efficient to stand your ground and stop a rusher in his tracks with a well-timed and well-placed straight lead. It's also a lot more fun.

As I mentioned at the beginning of this chapter, that straight punch will always beat an arced punch initiated at the same time—and sometimes even when the hook or swing is fired first. There's an excellent illustration of this in Haislet's *Boxing*, where it is also described as a way to defend against jabs. It makes such perfect sense to use the straight as a means of defense, Haislet noted that boxers often use it as such unconsciously regardless of whether or not they've be trained to do so.[30]

Part of what makes the straight lead such a great defensive move is the way in which it is thrown from the stance completely protects your centerline. In fact, unlike the rear cross or a conventional boxing jab, your target area actually becomes narrower as you throw the punch. This defensive property of the straight has its roots in fencing.

A fundamental principle of fencing is to "keep the line." By throwing a straight lead as a fencer would, you create a direct line from your shoulder to the arm. It is then very difficult for your opponent to get at you. Your centerline becomes unreachable as you extend your arm and turn your hip. You become that much harder to hit at the same time you are hitting. Talk about a win-win situation. According to Driscoll, the only way for your opponent to break through your straight lead defense is for you to stop throwing it.[31]

In this chapter, we've dipped a little into fighting science to explain the main reasons for using the straight punch: speed, accuracy, frequency of hits, balance, and safety. In the next chapter, I'll talk a bit more about application and how the straight lead can be used. In the meantime, just remember that Bruce wrote, "Into every Jeet Kune Do offense, defense is also welded in to form what I term 'defensive offense.'"[32]

"POWER IN THE PUNCH"

Before finishing this chapter on the advantages of the straight lead, I want to briefly return to the subject of biomechanics. We've already covered the how-to's and scientific whys related to the straight lead—the mechanics, laws governing physical motion, and so on. I'd just like to add one more piece of evidence in favor of the straight lead.

In 1974, *Black Belt* magazine reprinted Hayward Nishioka's study comparing the Jeet Kune Do straight lead to the karate punch. Electrodes were attached to the joints and the muscles around those joints. At the shoulder joint, the pectoralis major, the anterior deltoid, and latissimus dorsi were measured. At the shoulder girdle, the serratus anterior, trapezius II, and trapezius III were measured. And at the elbow joint, the biceps brachii, biceps brachialis, and triceps were measured. Muscle activity was measured using an electromyogram.

The Jeet Kune Do lead registered higher activity for all three muscles at the shoulder joint. The karate punch measured higher on all three muscles at the shoulder girdle. The most interesting finding, though, was at the elbow joint.

Remember the discussion of agonists and antagonists and how relaxation minimizes their simultaneous activation, resulting in a faster, more efficient, less fatiguing technique. Nishioka found that the karate punch activated *both* agonists and antagonists, "neutralizing the impact upon the punching glove." The antagonists—lats, traps, and biceps—contracted eccentrically "long before impact." Eccentric contraction is sometimes thought of as a "braking" contraction, and in this case, it clearly decreased the acceleration and effectiveness of the karate strike.

On the other hand, antagonist activity registered much lower with the JKD straight lead, resulting in a faster, and, consequently, more forceful punch (remember force equals mass times acceleration). Although agonists and antagonists were activated, simultaneous activation only occurred at the point of impact. This makes sense, considering the reasoning behind snappy punches. Just after impact is when we reverse directions and retract the hand, and this requires some eccentric contraction.[33, 34]

I've concluded this chapter with Nishioka's study to reiterate that proper technique, form, and relaxation result in the kind of speed and force that make all the advantages of the straight lead possible.

Notes

[1] Edwin L. Haislet, *Boxing* (New York: A.S. Barnes & Noble Company, 1940), p. 7.
[2] Bruce Lee, ed. John Little, *Jeet Kune Do: Bruce Lee's Commentaries on the Martial Way* (Boston: Tuttle Publishing, 1997), p. 212. These are the notes Bruce wrote on p. 6 in his copy of Haislet's book. He was essentially summarizing what Haislet had written on p. 7.
[3] Bruce Lee, ed. John Little, *The Tao of Gung Fu* (Boston: Tuttle Publishing., 1997, p. 59. Here you'll find earlier versions of these conclusions, showing that Bruce was investigating how to incorporate boxing principles of straight punching as early as 1964.

[4] Haislet, *Boxing*, p. 14. On straight punches versus swings: "They travel less distance than the round arm blows and will reach the mark first."

[5] Jim Driscoll, *The Straight Left and How To Cultivate It* (London: Athletic Publications, Ltd.), p. 40.

[6] Jack Dempsey, *Championship Fighting: Explosive Punching and Aggressive Defence* (New York: Prentice Hall, Inc., 1950), pp. 65–66. With the same common sense and geometrical reasoning as Driscoll, Dempsey wrote:

> A straight line is the shortest distance between two points. Either fist, in its normal punching position, has less distance to travel on a straight line to its target than on the curve of a hook or an uppercut. Consequently, a straight punch always should be used when (a) it has just as much chance of nailing the target as either of the others, and (b) when it will be just as explosive as either of the others. In other words, don't be taking long steps with hooks or uppercuts when you should be sharpshooting with straight punches.

[7] Roger Kahn, *A Flame of Pure Fire: Jack Dempsey and the Roaring '20's* (New York: Harcourt Brace, 1999, pp. 73–74. In describing Dempsey's scientific approach to shooting straight, biographer Roger Kahn explains how the educated punch will always win out over the uneducated one: "Try a roundhouse haymaker against a professional and you will neither land the blow nor remain upright through the next minute, let alone the round. The pro will beat you to the punch with a short left that he drives quickly and clinically inside your wild right."

[8] Lee, ed. John Little, *Jeet Kune Do: Bruce Lee's Commentaries on the Martial Way*, p. 210.

[9] Dempsey, *Championship Fighting: Explosive Punching and Aggressive Defense*, p. 49. Keep in mind that in Dempsey's case, the left is the lead hand:

> Contrary though it may seem, the *left* fist is more important for a *right-handed* fighter (not a southpaw) than is the *right fist*. That is true because, in normal punching position, the *left* hand is closer than the *right* to an opponent's head or body. Since it is closer, the *left* is harder for any opponent to avoid than the more distant *right*. If you can land solidly with a straight left or with a left hook, you'll generally knock your opponent off balance, at least, and "set him up" for a pot-shot with your right.

[10] Driscoll, *The Straight Left and How To Cultivate It*, p. 43. Written above the listed advantages of straight hitting in Bruce's copy of Haislet's book were the words "more economical both of time and effort." This was probably taken from page 43 of Driscoll's book.

[11] Ibid., p. 42.

[12] You'll find "balance is less disturbed" in Haislet, *Boxing*, p. 7.

[13] Driscoll, *The Straight Left and How To Cultivate It*, p. 59.

[14] Dempsey, *Championship Fighting: Explosive Punching and Aggressive Defence*, pp 32–33.

[15] Lee, ed. John Little, *Jeet Kune Do: Bruce Lee's Commentaries on the Martial Way*, pp 208, 257.

[16] Driscoll, *The Straight Left and How To Cultivate It*, p. 60. Driscoll wrote:

> In order to swing, a man must necessarily make his arm traverse a fairly lengthy
> arc in the air. He can scarcely fail to convey some intimation of the blow intended.
> In most cases it will only succeed in striking a target which is moving away—and
> it is surely scarcely necessary for me to point out that a blow of this kind is most
> unlikely to prove effective.

[17] Haislet, *Boxing* (New York: A.S. Barnes & Noble Company, 1940), p. 14.

[18] Driscoll, *The Straight Left and How To Cultivate It*, p. 41. With typical dry humor, Driscoll on swinging punches and their lack of accuracy:

> For quite apart from the loss of valuable time wasted by the swinging delivery, it
> is also practically impossible to aim a swing accurately. The swinger can only let
> one go in the hope that it will land there or thereabouts, while thanks partly to the
> time a swing occupies in starting and in delivery, the boxer who is temporarily fill-
> ing the role of a target, is given many more opportunities of avoiding its arrival.

[19] Richard Cohen, *By the Sword: A History of Gladiators, Musketeers, Samurai, Swashbucklers, and Olympic Champions* (New York: Random House, 2002), pp. 11–39.

[20] Driscoll, *The Straight Left and How To Cultivate It*, p. 20.

[21] Lee, ed. John Little, *Jeet Kune Do: Bruce Lee's Commentaries on the Martial Way*, p. 212.

[22] Haislet, *Boxing*, p. 14.

[23] Dempsey, *Championship Fighting: Explosive Punching and Aggressive Defence*, pp. 34–40. Dempsey devoted an entire chapter to the power line.

[24] Ibid, p. 39.

[25] Ibid. p. 42. Dempsey on the safety of straight punching:

> The old-time prize-fighters and boxers always made a practice of hitting straight,
> landing their punches fairly and squarely with the knuckles of the hand, and of
> thereby taking the jar of the impact on the part best fitted to support it. A swing-
> ing punch may land anyhow, and by no means infrequently with an open glove.
> It may arrive in such wise that only the thumb comes into contact with the head

of the body at which it is aimed—and in no possible instance can it arrive in such wise as to enable the pain or penalty of the impact to be properly distributed—as it should be—throughout the whole length of the arm. All the bones, sinews, and muscles of the hand and arm have been so placed by nature as to support the damaging effects of a hard punch when this is delivered straight and accurately, whereas the full jar of the impact of a swing has to be borne by the hand and wrist alone. The swinger's hands or wrists must go in time, and in short time at that. And this is surely an almost overwhelming argument in favour of the straight delivery as opposed to the swing.

[26] Captain John Godfrey ed. W.C. Heinz, "The Useful Science of Defence" in *The Fireside Book of Boxing* (New York: Simon and Schuster, 1961), pp. 158–162. You'll see this book in Bruce's library in John Little's *Bruce Lee: A Warrior's Journey*.

[27] Dempsey, *Championship Fighting: Explosive Punching and Aggressive Defence*, p. 11.

[28] Driscoll, *The Straight Left and How To Cultivate It*, p. 26.

[29] Dempsey, *Championship Fighting: Explosive Punching and Aggressive Defence*, pp. 115–116.

[30] Haislet, *Boxing*, p. 73. The following passage was underlined in Bruce Lee's copy, while the illustration appears on p. 78:

> *The Inside Parry and Left Jab*—is a straight left so timed as to take advantage of the opening left by the opponent's jab. It is a fundamental counter used consciously or unconsciously by almost every boxer. It is used to avoid the opponent's jab and at the same time sting and jar him. It is also used to "set up" openings for other counters. It is best used against a slow left jab.

[31] Driscoll, *The Straight Left and How To Cultivate It*, p. 30. Driscoll argued that the only way the straight lead could fail as a defensive weapon would be to stop using it:

> The fencer is taught to keep the line, and has to learn that nothing else matters so much as this. In fact, that nothing else really matters at all. For if the line be always preserved, he cannot be touched. And as with the fencer, so with the boxer. So long as the latter maintains his line, i.e., keeps that straight left of his shooting in and out, and his opponent at the business end of it. The other fellow will be powerless or practically powerless to do him any harm. One must either circumvent a straight left, or else force one's way through its defence, and the first of these feats can only be accomplished by compelling it to deviate from the straight line, or, in other words, to cease to be a straight left.

[32] Lee, ed. John Little, *Jeet Kune Do: Bruce Lee's Commentaries on the Martial Way*, p. 65.

[33] Hayward Nishioka, "Power in the Punch," *The Best of Bruce Lee*, 1974, pp. 72–74. Hayward Nishioka is the 1967 Pan-American Games Judo Gold Medalist, holds multiple degrees (one of which is a masters degree in physical education), and is an assistant professor at Los Angeles City College.

[34] M. Uyehara, *Bruce Lee: The Incomparable Fighter* (Santa Clarity, CA: Ohara Publications, Inc., 1988), p. 59. Unlike his relationship with other martial artists, it seems that of Bruce and Nishioka's was one of mutual and balanced respect.

CHAPTER SEVEN

APPLICATION

SPARRING

"**M**artial art" is an umbrella term that not only encompasses all disciplines relating to war, but all those pursuits that have evolved out of those disciplines into variations of sport (boxing and fencing), dance (forms competition), and exercise (tai chi, cardio kickboxing). It's important to remember, though, that when Bruce Lee spoke of martial art and Jeet Kune Do, he was referring to the original definition of "martial." He was talking about fighting.

Keep this in mind as we discuss how to apply the straight lead in combative situations. We are not dealing with point or touch scoring. Nor are we discussing rehearsed forms and drills. There's nothing wrong with studying in this way. The athleticism needed for katas, wushu competition, and film choreography is mind-boggling. These arts require elite-athlete skill, and anything that requires that kind of time, patience, and discipline is a worthwhile endeavor. They're just not close enough to their martial ancestors to fully appreciate the combative application of the straight lead.

In contrast to those other arts, Jeet Kune Do is not flashy, and there are very few techniques—a few punches and a few kicks. Remember the roots. Everything is based on efficiency and economy, and the straight lead is the epitome of efficiency. Blink and you might miss it. That's the point. In the heat of battle, there's no time for complicated techniques or wasted motion.

Figure 91: *Sparring is the only way to truly appreciate the straight lead. Here, I've used it to set up for the rear cross.*

Much of what Bruce Lee did on film was either an exaggerated version of Jeet Kune Do or, as in the case of weapons, was included for the benefit of making something look interesting for the camera. The techniques he wrote about and used for sparring at home, however, were much more streamlined than his movements for film.[1]

This brings us to the subject of sparring, which is another term that encompasses a broad range of definitions—from anything-goes fighting to choreographed routines. In JKD terms, however, sparring means getting closer to the real thing. This means donning training gloves and headgear. The restrictions and intensity level may vary. Sometimes you may train at less than your maximum intensity as you learn to incorporate specific techniques. At other times, you'll get closer to an all-out brawl.

In any case, the point of sparring is to teach you how to apply techniques in more realistic situations. Hitting focus pads is important, but focus pads don't hit back. You need to learn how to hit a moving target and land accurately. You'll also need to learn how to take a hit and counter. As Bruce himself pointed out, the only way to learn how to fight is to fight:

The best way to learn how to swim is to actually get into the water and swim; the best way to learn Jeet Kune Do is to spar. Only in free sparring can a practitioner begin to learn broken rhythm and the exact timing and correct judgment of distance.[2]

You'll see emphasis on these elements of time and distance over and over throughout fencing and boxing literature. Mastery of these variables is the difference between dry-land swimming and diving into the water.

"THE STRAIGHT PUNCH IS THE CORE OF JEET KUNE DO"

We began this book with the statement that the straight lead is the core of JKD, and from the last chapter on the advantages of straight punching it's easy to see why. In this chapter, I'll talk about how to strategically use the lead hand. The emphasis Bruce placed on the lead hand comes from boxing, where it is "the central theme."[3] All other techniques are set up by or follow the straight lead, and the stance that I spent so much time explaining has been set up specifically for delivery of the straight lead.

"THE ESSENCE OF FIGHTING IS THE ART OF MOVING AT THE RIGHT TIME"[4]

STRATEGIC VARIABLES

The way fighters play with time is very similar to the way musicians interpret time. You can play on the beat, behind the beat, or syncopate. Staccato or legato. You can choose to play or let the rhythm section pass you by. The tempo may vary from adagio (slow) to allegro (quick). To the time, you can then add dynamic variations—pianissimo (soft), mezzo forte (moderately loud), or fortissimo (very loud).

Fighting has analogous variables. The difference between notes played staccato (rapid and clipped) and legato (smooth and slurred) is the difference between a snappy punch that minimally penetrates the target, barely touching it, and a slower power punch that penetrates the target with greater depth. You can throw out a punch and then pause—choosing not to play and letting the rhythm section pass beneath you—and then throw out another punch. Tempo is something that is referred to as cadence in the martial arts, particularly in fencing. And dynamics may be thought of as variations in intensity instead of volume. You might think of the difference between pianissimo and fortissimo as the difference between a feeler jab and a stiff one.

And then, of course, you can mix and match these variables. You can play or punch staccato and forte. Or adagio and pianissimo. Legato and fortissimo. The point is you can throw a single punch in so many different ways, and by doing so, you keep your opponent guessing.

PUNCHING DEPTH

We just touched on the subject of varying the depth to your punches. Bruce referred to this as "short" versus "long" punches.[5] Short punches are those that shoot out quickly but barely touch or minimally penetrate the target. Long punches are those slower but more forceful ones that punch further through the target. Having control over the depth of your punches, again, keeps your opponent guessing and enables you to disrupt his rhythm. If you throw a series of short punches and throw in a long one, your opponent won't expect it. You can also do the opposite: throw a series of long punches and then set him off-balance and upset his rhythm with a short one.[6]

It's important to note that not every punch you throw should be with the same force or depth. Mixing it up adds more tools to your arsenal. And throwing a short punch is much faster than throwing a long one. If it's the difference between stinging your opponent with a fast, short straight lead or missing altogether with a slow haymaker, I'll take that stinging jab.

You can practice depth control with the focus mitts or the heavy bag. Practice hitting with varying degrees of depth. Try hitting as forcefully as you can, going all the way through the target. Then try barely touching the target. Or pull back without hitting the target at all. That's control.

One thing to watch for here is that many people mistake depth and force for speed. When asked to barely touch the target, they think they are hitting "lighter" and so they slow down, too. Don't do that! If you intend to do some kind of damage—I'm not talking about the feeler jab here—you want to hit with the same speed with *every* punch. Remember, force equals mass times acceleration, so do not slow down.

Another purpose of varying the depth of your punches is that it allows you to bridge the gap to your opponent. By throwing a series of short straight leads, you can keep your opponent on the defensive as you get closer to him. Even if you fail to reach him, you are now close enough to follow up with a long lead or other weapons.[7]

TIMING

BROKEN RHYTHM

The introduction of the short and long punches segues nicely into the subjects of timing and broken rhythm. Again, this is something taken from fencing strategy. The idea is that you establish a rhythm with the lead hand by throwing out a series of punches with the same depth and speed, maybe at the same target, for it is human nature to be set in a trance by rhythm.[8]

Bruce addressed this trancelike state and how it relates to fighting:

> A series of judiciously slowed down feints to the leg and slow gaining and break-ing ground may be used (to 'put the opponent to sleep'). A final simple move-ment which suddenly erupts at highest speed will often take him unawares.[9]

You'll find the principle of broken rhythm in JKD has its roots in fencing and the writings of Julio Martinez Castello:

> Timing consists of selecting the opportune moment for making an attack or a parry. This opportune moment usually has to be created rather than discovered . . . The movements of the attacking and defending blades work almost in rhythm with each other, and although there is a slight advantage in the initiative of the attack, it must also be backed by superior speed in order to land successfully. However, when this rhythm is broken, speed is no longer the primary element in the success of the attack or counter attack of the man who has broken the rhythm. If the rhythm has been well established, there is a tendency to continue in the sequence of the movement. In other words, each man is motor-set to continue the sequence of the movements. The man who can beat this rhythm by a slight hesitation or an unex-pected movement can now score an attack or counter attack with only moderate speed; for his opponent is motor-set to continue with the previous rhythm, and before he can adjust himself to the change, he has been hit.[10]

Castello noted that by properly timing your opponent with broken rhythm, you do not have to be particularly fast to be effective. Similarly, Driscoll said that a properly timed straight lead may drop an opponent with seemingly little effort, particularly if he's advancing toward you. In this case, he is being hit not only with your force, but the force of his own advance as well.[11] Impeccable timing is the mark of an educated, smart fighter, and to a certain extent, timing can compensate for a lack in speed and size.[12]

Trancelike state, "put to sleep," "motor-set." You want to lull your opponent into a state of comfort and then suddenly strike. Also know that you can do this either by slowly setting a rhythm of advancing and then following with a quick advance. Or you can set up a rhythm of retreat and then suddenly step forward to intercept his advance or attack. Which brings us to the subject of the stop-hit.

THE STOP-HIT

There are really only two ways to bridge the gap between you and your opponent—either you go to him, or he comes to you. In the case of the stop-hit, your opponent is coming to you. Your opponent provides the distance. We've already touched on the idea of "defensive offense."[13] The stop-hit is the hallmark of defensive offense and is often used as a way to stop an attack dead in its tracks. But it can also be set up by motor-setting your opponent as just discussed.

Like many key elements of JKD, the stop-hit also has its roots in fencing. Upon introducing the stop-hit, Nadi wrote, "Here then you have the first glimpse of one of the fundamental fencing dogmas, to wit, that *the best moment of attack from immobility is when your opponent advances toward you.*"[14]

Driscoll was quick to draw the parallels between the fencing stop-hit and boxing strategy.[15] Like Nadi, Driscoll knew that an opponent is most vulnerable when attacking and that aggressive rushers are easily dealt with by a well-timed, straight lead stop-hit, what he referred to as "the stop policy":

> Perhaps the most effective defensive straight left-handed "stop" is that which is, or should be employed, against the determined rushes or persistently attacking opponent. For these men are, after all, the easiest men in the world to beat at the boxing game.[16]

Once someone has committed to an attack, there's no turning back.[17] Reversing directions during an attack is not recommended. This puts your opponent in an even more vulnerable spot. Of course, with correct timing, you're going to get him anyway.

THREE WAYS TO TIME

It's worth noting there are really three points where you can time your opponent. First is before he or she attacks. Bruce referred to this as attack on preparation. This is more of a mental cue than a physical one, for your opponent has not yet made a movement toward you. You may catch him, though, mentally preparing for attack, and at this moment, his defenses are down.[18]

The second place for you to attack is during your opponent's attack. This would be the stop-hit. With a fast and straight lead punch, you may beat your opponent's attack even if you start yours after your opponent's is initiated.

Finally, you may attack after your opponent's completed his offensive as he's retracting his hand. He is still in no position to relaunch an attack, and if he's slow to recover to the on-guard position, you have even more time to get to him.

STEP-IN, STEP-OUT

Another way to catch your opponent in a stop-hit is by the step-in-step-out feint.[19] We've already talked about setting up rhythms by advancing slowly and then quickly advancing or by retreating and then suddenly advancing. The step-in-step-out is a little bit of both. Set up a pattern of stepping toward him and then stepping away. Once you've lulled him into a pattern, break it by stepping in and instead of stepping out, this time quickly step in again and attack.

THE HALF-BEAT

Broken rhythm, stop-hits, time thrusts, the step-in-step-out feint, and other attacks and counterattacks are all made possible by what Ted Wong calls half-beat footwork. Once again, this has its origins in fencing strategy. Nadi described the half-beat and how it links offense and defense:

> Actually, these "paradoxes" are the basis upon which the entire art and science of arms is built. In combat, when the fencer forsakes the orthodox attack and parry-riposte for the counterattack, he literally puts the half-note into the music of fencing, superimposing it upon, or obliterating temporarily, the whole-note concept and rhythm. In fact, the stronger the fencer the greater the importance of, and the results obtained by, this half-note. This is so true that the champion succeeds in mixing his offensive and defensive operations to such a large degree—passing from one to the other so rapidly—that even for the most competent judge it is sometimes impossible to analyze his intentions and actions correctly.[20]

We already addressed the half-beat in the footwork chapter. Again, a whole note consists of both the landing of your front and rear foot. That's one full beat. Many martial arts only have whole-beat footwork and may appear very rigid. Fighters of such arts can only make another move once an entire beat has been completed.

But by being able to reverse direction and change from defense to offense on the half-beat, fencers have many more variables to play with. There are many more opportunities to trick an opponent and set him up by disrupting his rhythm. He will always be guessing.

If you are able to move on the half-beat in any direction, you become unpredictable and much more mobile, exponentially creating striking opportunities. You can only take advantage of the half-beat and its benefits, though, through sound, precise footwork.

DISTANCE

As you'll recall from the footwork chapter, maintaining proper distance—or the fighting measure—is crucial to landing punches. Obviously, you don't want to be too far away from your opponent, because you'll never reach him. You also don't want to be too close, or you'll jam yourself and lose leverage. Remember we always want to have about 3 or 4 inches to punch through the target—no more, no less.

When in an actual combative situation, though, we find it can be pretty difficult hitting a moving target, especially one that doesn't present many opportunities for countering with stop-hits. This is where the straight lead comes in. As mentioned before, throwing a combination of straight punches keeps your opponent on the defense, allowing you to get within striking range.

Again, you can use all those combinations of short and long punches. Double jabs. Triple jabs. You can also vary the targets of those straight punches. Maybe shoot low and then high. Or double jab high and drop shift low. I'll go over variations of the straight lead later, but an example of using straight lead variations is to throw a backfist and straight and then finish up with a corkscrew hook. The point is that you can be very creative with just the lead hand, and this allows you to work your way in toward your opponent. This is how you bridge the gap.

Also know that lead hand combos are much quicker than combos using the rear hand. This has to do with the advanced position of the front hand and the fact that throwing a rear hand requires greater deviation from the stance. And more deviation from the stance means slower recovery time and an overall slower combination. See Figure 92.

FIVE WAYS OF ATTACK

We've got some new toys in our straight lead tool bag now. Broken rhythm, short punches, long punches, half-beats, step-in-step-out feints, stop-hits, timing, distance. If you're familiar with Bruce Lee's writings, then you already know there are five ways of attack. I'm just going to briefly touch on each one to explain where some of our new tools fit in. For more information on the five ways of attack, be sure to consult the *Tao of Jeet Kune Do*.

Figure 92: *Playing with time and distance creates striking opportunities.*

SIMPLE ANGLE ATTACK (SAA)

The simple angle attack is a one-motion attack. In most cases, it's the straight lead, although kicks and other punches may be used for SAA as well. This is a one-shot deal, and so it is the most difficult method of attack, requiring precise distance, timing, and lightning speed. You must be in optimal position to execute a simple angle attack, and this is always accomplished through footwork.[21, 22]

APPLICATION

ATTACK BY COMBINATION (ABC)

Attack by combination is exactly as it's named. A combination of punches are thrown—often to more than one line—in an attempt to create an opening for a finishing blow.[23] Most of the time, such combinations lead with the straight punch (see Figures 93 through 96). Here are some examples:

- Straight right/left cross/right hook
- Straight right/straight right/corkscrew hook
- Straight right/left uppercut/right hook
- Straight right drop shift/right hook to the head
- Straight right/right hook low/right hook high

You get the idea. You can then start adding the elements of time and broken rhythm to this. Vary the depth of your punches. Add stutter steps and pauses between shots. Even with only a few punches, the possibilities are endless.

To experiment with time, try only throwing triple straight leads and vary your combinations by time and depth only:

- Short/short/long
- Short/long/short
- Short/short/short
- Long/short/short
- Long/long/short
- Long/long/long
- Long/short/long
- Short/short/pause/long
- Long/pause/short/short
- Short/pause/long/long

Again, the combinations are endless. Always keep in mind that you do not need a lot of techniques to keep your opponent guessing. It's not how many techniques you have in your tool bag, it's what you can do with those tools. Again, knowing the ins and outs of a few techniques is preferable to only superficially knowing an entire catalog of technique.

Figure 93: *The straight lead is the best way to set up combinations.*

Figure 94: *Follow the straight with a rear cross.*

Figure 95: *And then a hook kick . . .*

Figure 96*: . . . or a side kick.*

PROGRESSIVE INDIRECT ATTACK (PIA)

The progressive indirect attack is sometimes thought of as "attack by fraud," because it is begins with a feint or fake or uncommitted strike, making this an indirect attack. The purpose of the PIA is to bridge the gap, to cover distance against an opponent who is unreachable with a single direct attack. Varying your punching depth is an example of PIA. You may throw two short punches knowing full well that you won't reach your opponent, but those short punches allow you to bridge the gap. They allow you to work your way in and then deliver a blow. Hence the name "progressive." Bridging the gap is a progression of steps to get to the opposition.

The feint, fake, or uncommitted jab draw your opponent's attention, allowing you to work into striking distance. I'll discuss this later in the chapter, but remember that you cannot use PIA effectively with a weak straight lead. If your opponent thinks your straight is powderpuffery, he or she won't fall for your fakes or feints. And if your opponent knows that your lead hand poses no threat, he or she will be more likely to counter your every move.

ATTACK BY DRAWING (ABD)

Attack by drawing is actually a secondary attack. You are tricking or luring your opponent into launching an attack so that you may counter, usually with a stop-hit. You set him up. Remember, your opponent is at his most vulnerable once he has committed to an attack. Mentally, he is not thinking about defense. Physically, any offensive movement is going to leave an opening for you somewhere. Also remember how difficult and dangerous it is to try to change direction in the midst of an attack.

The best part of ABD, though, is that because you are setting up your opponent, you can easily predict his attack and counter safely. ABD is dependent on distance and timing. You deliberately make yourself open and appear vulnerable. How you do this, again, allows you to predict what he will do. By giving your opponent what appears to be a particular opening, you actually control the attacks he might choose while eliminating other possibilities.

Again, the success of ABD is almost entirely contingent on timing and distance. You must have precise control of distance, knowing just how much should be enough to safely lure the opposition. And when he makes an advance, you must be able to time him. The half-beat, the stop-hit, and the step-in-step-out feint are all tools for implementing ABD. When we discuss the variations of the straight lead, you'll see how position of the lead hand can be used to lure your opponent as well.

HAND IMMOBILIZATION ATTACK

With hand immobilization attack, you immobilize your opponent by force by trapping. In JKD, this is one of the last vestiges of Wing Chun and even then, it is used less than the other methods of attack. As with everything else in JKD, trapping techniques must be kept simple to be effective. It's beyond the scope of this book to really discuss trapping, but keep in mind that whatever trapping techniques you use must also be accompanied by appropriate footwork. This is what set Lee's trapping technique apart from others.[24]

Remember, as discussed earlier, that in the latter stages of JKD development, Bruce had come to the conclusion that more traditional fighting elements, like trapping, were not that effective in actual combat. It was essentially the shortcomings of traditional techniques that propelled him to develop JKD. Wing Chun, for example, requires both fighters to set up so that their arms are touching. The system is based on touch sensitivity. But in a real situation, it's unlikely that someone is going to leave his arm out for you so you can set up properly. If the other guy's unwilling to play your game, you're out of luck.

Bruce makes a statement about traditional styles in his fight scene with Bob Wall in *Enter the Dragon*. The two square off in a traditional position with their forearms touching. But instead of engaging in a lot of blocking and unnecessary movement, what does Bruce do? BAM! He throws a straight lead and whacks Bob—twice. Why waste time when you can launch the most direct attack? It's no mistake that the two start from a close combat set up either. Bruce is proving that he can beat the trappers at their own game without having to actually engage in trapping. Knowing a few simple trapping techniques may be useful if you choose to play the game, but the straight lead gets the job done quicker.

Of course, as Nadi emphasized, to execute the simplest, most direct attack requires tremendous speed, and this is what eventually enabled Bruce to abandon Wing Chun. To really appreciate the scene from *Enter the Dragon*, you'll have to watch it frame by frame, because Bruce was so incredibly fast. You'll see that the straight lead is deceptively simple. It takes years to develop the necessary muscle memory, alignment, footwork, and mechanics that collectively contribute to speed and power. It takes years to hone something that is, for the most part, imperceptible to the untrained eye. See Figures 97 through 99.

Figure 97: *Playing the trapping game. I throw out a finger jab that is blocked by my opponent.*

Figure 98: *As I'm being blocked, I immediately trap his arm and throw a straight lead.*

Figure 99: *Even in close quarters, I've used footwork to bridge the gap and properly execute the punch. The alignment and mechanics are the same. The only difference is the distance covered, which is regulated by my back foot.*

HIT FIRST, HIT HARD, HIT OFTEN

The five ways of attack are of little use to us if we do not immediately establish the validity of the straight lead. You must let your opponent know from the get go that your lead hand is dangerous, a threat. Make him respect you. Pop him a few times right off the bat with that rapier-like straight lead. Once he knows you can hit him—and from a disconcerting distance—the rest is a piece of cake. From that moment on, he will react, even flinch, whenever you make a move. If you feint, he'll fall for it. If you throw a short jab, he'll be put off balance in anticipation of a more damaging blow. Then he's a sitting duck for whatever punch with which you care to follow up.

But you can only take advantage of this if you have a strong lead. This is why it's so important to have the mechanics down. You've got to be able to generate force and let the opposition feel it. As Dempsey wrote, the timid, light lead jab, is of little value in the ring:

> Any time you extend your left fist for a tap or for an all-out punch, you're taking a gamble on being nailed with a counter-punch . . . an opponent who is defending only against taps and slaps will be much more alert to counter than will an opponent who is being *bombed*.[25]

So, remember with the straight lead we want to *bomb*. Driscoll had a similar theory regarding the straight. It must be technically sound and damaging before it can be used strategically:

> For no matter how straightly it may be used, nor how frequently it may shoot out, the left punch is of precious little use as an offensive weapon, and even absolutely useless as a defensive one unless it is capable of checking an attack and even of *stopping* most attacks. I would give the same advice to boxers as that which Lord Fisher laid down as the rule to be obeyed in all naval combats, viz., to hit first, hit hard, and hit often, with the addendum that they should always, or practically always, "hit straight."[26]

The progressive indirect attack and certainly the single direct attack are only possible with a deadly lead hand.[27]

THE PARADOX OF SIMPLICITY

We've just discussed the more advanced concepts of timing and distance, but I'd like to reiterate the emphasis Bruce placed on simplicity, because now we are talking about application. When you are placed in an actual combative situation, the abstract concept of simplicity becomes glaringly concrete. I never fully appreciated the straight lead until I started to spar. Its design, mechanics, and how it lends itself to instinctual use suddenly made perfect sense.

Now I understand when Bruce wrote, "When the student begins to spar, then he will stop searching for the accumulation of techniques; rather he will devote the needed hours of practice to the simple technique for its *right execution*."[28] For so-called JKD practitioners who insist on the endless accumulation of techniques, I can only guess that they do not spar. For in the heat of battle, there is no time to think. The more steps needed for an attack, the more time is wasted in thought. The flashier the technique, the more time is wasted making excess motion.

According to Bruce, simplicity is what makes an attack unbeatable: "There is no effective trick to stop a properly timed simple attack, and always remember the best technique in offense or defense is the simple one properly performed."[29] *No* way to stop a good simple attack. And there is no simpler attack than popping your opponent with a single straight lead. See Figure 100.

Figure 100: *It doesn't get any simpler than this. As your opponent moves in to attack, throwing a perfectly timed straight is, all at once, both the perfect defensive and offensive move.*

The irony, of course, is that the simplest punch is actually the most difficult to master. As Nadi wrote, "The simplest of all attacks is the straight thrust. Because of its simplicity, this attack is the most difficult to execute in combat. To be successful, it requires perfect timing, exact distance, and tremendous speed."[30]

This is the paradox of simplicity. The simpler your attack, the more crucial the elements of timing and distance become. And as we've already seen, achieving the necessary speed, which requires maximum efficiency, depends on excellent form and precise mechanics. This is what Bruce Lee meant when he spoke of "daily decrease." Your aim should not be to complicate existing techniques or acquire new ones. True mastery is a process of constant refinement, and as you approach technical perfection, you approach absolute simplicity.

NOTES

[1] In conversation with Ted Wong, March 18, 2004.

[2] Bruce Lee, ed. John Little, *Jeet Kune Do: Bruce Lee's Commentaries on the Martial Way* (Boston: Tuttle Publishing, 1997), p.25.

[3] Ibid., p. 207.

[4] Ibid., p. 249.

[5] Ibid., p. 115. Bruce talked about varying the depth of punching as a form of feinting:

The first movement (feint)—must be long and deep (by that I mean penetrating) to draw the parry. He second real movement (attack) must be fast and decisive allowing the defender no possibility of recovery—long-short; even in the delivery of attack with two feints, the depth of the first feint must force the opponent to move to the Defence—long-short-short.

[6] In conversation with Ted Wong. June 18, 2004.

[7] Lee, ed. John Little, *Jeet Kune Do: Bruce Lee's Commentaries on the Martial Way*, p. 99.

[8] Simon Frith, *Performing Rites: On the Value of Popular Music* (Cambridge, MA: Harvard University Press, 1996), pp. 145–157. Frith reviews some fascinating theories on rhythm and human nature:

> Satie's concept of furniture music (like Brian Eno's idea of "music for airports") is more complex than it might at first seem. There are images of both culture and nature here (a chair, casual conversation; heat and light), the suggestion both that music shapes itself, usefully, to bodily needs, and that individual bodies are themselves absorbed into a kind of implacable sonic flow. Virtual time here describes an experience of bodilessness, an indifference to materiality (minimal composers have a declared interest in Eastern religions), and Mertens notes the paradox that rhythmic regularity may well have exactly the same effect in dance music: disco, he suggests, also works like a "narcotic," "individuating" musical experience through repetition but leaving the listener/dancer "floating in cosmic soup," with no aims, no desires at all.

[9] Lee, ed. John Little, *Jeet Kune Do: Bruce Lee's Commentaries on the Martial Way*, p. 107.

[10] Julio Martinez Castello, *The Theory and Practice of Fencing* (New York: Charles Scribner's Sons, 1933), pp. 56–57. You'll find quotes from this passage in Bruce Lee, *Tao of Jeet Kune Do* (Santa Clarita, CA, Ohara Publications, Inc., 1975), p. 62.

[11] Jim Driscoll, *The Straight Left and How To Cultivate It* (London: Athletic Publications, Ltd.), pp. 57–58.

[12] Lee, ed. John Little, *Jeet Kune Do: Bruce Lee's Commentaries on the Martial Way*, p. 99.

[13] Ibid., 65.

[14] Aldo Nadi, *On Fencing*, (Bangor, ME: Laureate Press, 1994), p. 88. Similarly, in Lee, ed. John Little, *Jeet Kune Do: Bruce Lee's Commentaries on the Martial Way*, p. 187, Bruce wrote, "The best moment to attack from immobility is when your opponent advances toward you."

[15] Driscoll, *The Straight Left and How To Cultivate It*, p. 56.

[16] Ibid., pp. 64–65.

[17] Lee, ed. John Little, *Jeet Kune Do: Bruce Lee's Commentaries on the Martial Way*, p. 105. Bruce argued that a man cannot give equal attention to offense and defensive simultaneously: "An excellent moment to launch an attack is when the opponent is himself preparing an attack. His intention and hand movement will then be momentarily concentrated more on attack than defense."

[18] Ibid., p. 100.

[19] Ibid., 249.

[20] Nadi, *On Fencing*, p. 183.

[21] Ibid., p. 89.

[22] Lee, *Tao of Jeet Kune Do*, p. 194.

[23] Ibid., p. 197.

[24] In conversation with Ted Wong, June 8, 2004.

[25] Jack Dempsey, *Championship Fighting: Explosive Punching and Aggressive Defence* (New York: Prentice Hall, Inc., 1950), p. 51.

[26] Driscoll, *The Straight Left and How To Cultivate It*, p. 80.

[27] Lee, ed. John Little, *Jeet Kune Do: Bruce Lee's Commentaries on the Martial Way*, p. 213. Bruce declared, "The right lead is the opening gambit in any hand combat."

[28] John R. Little, *Bruce Lee: A Warrior's Journey* (Chicago: Contemporary Books, 2001), p. 115.

[29] Lee, ed. John Little, *Jeet Kune Do: Bruce Lee's Commentaries on the Martial Way*, p. 66.

[30] Nadi, *On Fencing*, p. 89.

SPEED

According to Nadi, "In all attacks, and particularly composed ones, the simpler the action the greater the speed of both blade and body must be. The initial speed of the body should, therefore, be in direct proportion to the simplicity or complexity of the action."[1] As we've stressed in the last chapter, the straight lead, and more specifically, the single direct attack, is the simplest, and therefore, most difficult of all attacks. Its simplicity makes it paradoxically the attack that calls for the highest skill level, and speed is at the top of the list of skills required. The subject of speed, then, warrants having its own little chapter.

Bruce Lee wrote that the two main components of speed were recognition and reaction. He then further broke it down into five separate components: perceptual, mental, initiation, performance, and alteration.[2]

PERCEPTUAL SPEED

This is essentially how fast you can recognize a movement or striking opportunity. It is, for the most part, visual, although auditory cues may sometimes be helpful. Perceptual speed is how fast you can see or recognize an attack to speedily evade or how fast you can see an opening giving you the advantage when striking. Ted Wong remarked that Bruce would just watch people to develop his skills of perception—how they run, walk, swing their arms, even how they'd hold a fork.[3] Training for perceptual speed is training your eye to see things quickly.

Figure 101: *The simpler the punch, the greater the required speed.*

Vision awareness can compensate, to a certain extent, for a slow delivery, and the good news is that it's something you can cultivate.[4] One helpful hint is not to focus on any one area of the target. I don't know where this myth came from about fixing your gaze on your opponent's eyes. Maybe a quick glance, but your opponent's not going to hit you with his or her eyes! Instead use your peripheral vision to try to get a sense of the position of your opponent's entire body. Take in your opponent from head to toe without focusing on any one point. "A habit of diffusing the attention over a wider area," Bruce wrote, "helps the offensive passer to see openings more quickly."[5] By doing so, you'll be able to detect both kicks and punches and from which side they'll originate. A shoulder twitch. A slight wind-up. Train your eyes to detect the smallest movements, and you'll be able to anticipate and counter your opponent much more effectively.

MENTAL SPEED

Ted Wong believes that 70 percent of speed is mental, and only 30 percent is physical. Mental speed, according to the *Tao*, is how quickly your mind chooses a particular movement.[6] The irony here, though, is that at the highest speeds, there is no mental effort being exerted. Or we should say, there is no *conscious* mental effort. The highest stage of any art is that state of "no mindedness."

To achieve this, there are several things that must be in place. First, you must keep your arsenal of weapons to a minimum. As I mentioned in the last chapter, the fewer choices you have to rifle through, the faster you will be. Take a few of the most effective weapons, and keep it simple. The straight lead or thrust, as Driscoll and Nadi have mentioned, is the simplest attack or counter. When it has been learned properly, its simplicity lends itself to instinctual use. Remember:

> Speed of perception is somewhat affected by the distribution of the observer's attention—fewer separate choices, faster action. When the cue to be recognized is likely to be one of several, each of which requires a different response, the time is lengthened. *Choice reaction takes longer than simple reaction.* This is the basis for training the tools in terms of *neurophysiological adjustment* toward *instinctive economy.* Instinctive movement, being the simplest, is the quickest and most accurate.[7]

You must also train your nervous system. We've already talked about neuromuscular programming. With hours of proper programming, you will reach a state where you do not have to think about form, or sequence, or even distance and timing. Your body will know.

This goes hand in hand with form and mechanics. As Bruce wrote, "Many fighters fail to appreciate how much true speed depends on *economy of motion* (i.e., good form and good coordination)."[8] Remember the stance itself was designed for optimal speed and minimal deviation when making a motion. This also why we punch straight. It requires less distance to reach the target, and therefore, less time. A swinging punch must travel a greater distance and takes more time.

Once you're in the proper stance, remember the sequence of movement and mechanics. If you are unable to perform these correctly, you will sacrifice a great deal of speed. Remember when practicing—do *not* skip steps or gloss over mechanics. You will be programming your nervous system incorrectly, and it takes much more time to deprogram yourself than it does to get the technique right the first time around. Go slowly. Take the time to learn things correctly, and this will pay off. Someday, when you need it, that technique and speed will be at your fingertips, and you won't have to think about it. Remember what Bruce said in *Enter the Dragon:* "I do not hit. It hits all by itself." This is how we define mental speed.

Don't forget that one of the most important mental factors contributing to speed is relaxation. Relax, Max! First, being physically relaxed keeps you from unnecessarily tensing muscles not used in the technique. If you're tense, upon perceiving an opportunity, you must first relax the tensed muscles before you can move. You lose valuable milliseconds, or even seconds, that way.

Second, mental tension may cloud your head, because you're consciously thinking too much. For your straight lead to "hit all by itself," you cannot be thinking.

INITIATION SPEED

Initiation speed is how quickly you can overcome inertia. The stance is especially important here, because, as defined by Bruce, initiation speed requires "economical starting from the right posture."[9] When we think of speed, we generally think of something moving really fast externally. But to truly understand speed, we also have to look at the bigger picture. To throw a fast straight lead, for example, you must first push off the left leg. To push off with maximum acceleration, you must start from the proper stance.

Remember our discussion of body feel. Again, this is something you cannot see. But you need to feel all of that potential energy bottled up. You should feel the potential energy stored on the medial sides of your legs, concentrated on the ball of your left foot. Feel your upper body coiled and ready to whip out at the hip. These are all contributors to initiation speed, and they can only be achieved from a properly constructed stance. When you are in the stance, you should feel ready to unleash a lightning bolt at any given moment.

Once you have grasped the principles of a correct stance and your body is able to feel them, I suggest you take a look at the stances of other fighters. What are they doing right? Wrong? Do you think they'll be fast? Slow? When you know how a proper stance feels, you can train your eye to see such things. You'll have a better idea of what to expect from a fighter just by observing his or her stance.

PERFORMANCE SPEED

Performance is the actual movement. If initiation speed is largely internal, performance speed is the external movement that you can actually see. It goes without saying that performance speed is dependent on precise mechanics and the proper sequence. Every step is equally important, from the initial push-off to the retraction of the hand. I sound like a broken record by now, but performance speed is developed by neuromuscular programming—in other words, practice, practice, practice. There's no other way to program those neuromuscular pathways.

Performance speed, by the way, applies not only to the single straight lead, but also to combinations as well. To perform combinations effectively, you must smoothly transition from technique to technique. This is dependent on coordination of mechanics, footwork, and weight transfer.

ALTERATION SPEED

Alteration speed is how quickly you can change direction in mid-motion. You already know that it's incredibly difficult, if not downright dangerous, to stop a punch once you've committed to throwing it. This is why fighters are so vulnerable to counters. Alteration speed requires a great deal of skill. You need it to throw combos and to take advantage of all the strategic tools like broken rhythm, the stop and go, the step-in-step-out feint. To change up speed and/or direction requires an extremely high level of coordination, for any excessive motion will slow you down. Swing too wide and you have that much more distance to recover before you're ready to fire again. As with the other types of speed, you must think precision and economy, economy, economy.

NOTES

[1] Aldo Nadi, *On Fencing*, (Bangor, ME: Laureate Press, 1994), p. 151.

[2] Bruce Lee, *Tao of Jeet Kune Do* (Santa Clarita, CA, Ohara Publications, Inc., 1975), pp. 56–59.

[3] In conversation with Ted Wong, March 8, 2004.

[4] Lee, *Tao of Jeet Kune Do*, p. 54. While muscle contraction is determined by genetically determined fast twitch fibers, Bruce believed vision training could make up for what we fail to inherit, saying, "A boy who is a little slow in reaction time, or in speed of delivery, may compensate for this slowness through quick seeing."

[5] Ibid., p. 55.

[6] Ibid., p. 57.

[7] Ibid., p. 55.

[8] Ibid., p. 57.

[9] Ibid., p. 57.

VARIATIONS OF THE STRAIGHT PUNCH

Within the realm of form and mechanics, we've only covered what I like to call the "pure straight lead," that is, the straight lead delivered at its fastest without compromising force production. This is the backbone of JKD and is the punch you will throw most often, but in certain situations, it will be more appropriate to throw a variation of the straight. Those variations include the corkscrew hook, backfist, and shovel hook.

There are, of course, other punches in JKD that act as supporting players like the hook, uppercut, and rear cross. As I've said before, there are very few punches in JKD. In fact, I've listed them all already—the straight, cross, hook, uppercut, backfist, corkscrew, shovel hook. But once again, simplicity is deceptive. Between a pure straight and a pure hook lies an entire continuum of punches that includes a blend of both. We won't be able to go into too much detail with this continuum, but this concept should help you to understand the first variation of the straight, the corkscrew hook.

THE CORKSCREW HOOK

There are a couple of instances when it is better to throw a corkscrew hook instead of a pure straight lead. The first is if your target circles to your left side (counterclockwise). To hit him in time, before he can move again, you will have to pivot step to get to him.

To throw a corkscrew hook, start from the regular on-guard position. As you shoot out, though, you will actually raise your elbow and turn your palm over. Remember, you do not do this when a target is directly in front of you. That's when you use a straight. The corkscrew is used when the target is to your left. Your elbow should be up, giving you extra torque into the target and a downward trajectory as well. And always, always, always land the target with the bottom three knuckles.

Figure 102: *Keeping the front hand low is not the fastest way to throw a straight lead, but it gives you more options to throw other punches and keeps your opponent guessing.*

The pivot step, which can be traced to Dempsey's book, is crucial to the corkscrew, because you will need to redirect your body weight toward the target, which is now toward your left. Remember, you always want your hip pointing toward the target, because that means the majority of your body weight, your trunk, is headed in the desired direction.[1] See Figures 103 through 105.

Because you are angling to your right (counterclockwise), your power line changes, so you will actually hit with the palm down. You can test this theory with the heavy bag. Try throwing a straight with the thumb up as you circle the bag to your right. Feels pretty awkward, right? Now try pivoting to the right and throw straights with your palm down. You should feel much more solid with your elbow up and palm down. This is the only case when it is advantageous to land a blow with the palm down, and this has to do with the angle and your body structure.[2]

Figure 103: *The corkscrew hook from on guard.*

Figure 104: *As your hand shoots out, you must also pivot step.*

Figure 105: *At impact, your palm is down and your elbow should angle up.*

So, again, one instance in which you would use the corkscrew would be to hit a target that is high and slightly to your left. The other would be if you were too close to the target to throw an effective straight. The pure straight lead is a long-range punch used for a one-shot deal or to bridge the gap to the opposition. It must be thrown from an optimal distance to be effective. If you are too close to the target, you lose leverage and end up pushing instead of forcefully striking. To maintain leverage at close range, then, you can throw a corkscrew hook. Raising your elbow allows you to "angle up," In this way, you optimize your leverage and avoid jamming yourself.   See Figures 106 and 107.

There are varying degrees of angling up. At its most extreme, you are almost throwing a hook, so the corkscrew may be used when your hand is positioned slightly to the right of where it would be in the normal stance. At the other end of the spectrum, you may nearly throw a straight with a slight corkscrew twist. The corkscrew lies somewhere in the middle on the straight-hook continuum.

Figure 106: *Side view of corkscrew hook from the stance.*

Figure 107: *Side view of pivot stepping and angling up for the corkscrew hook.*

THE BACKFIST

If you use the corkscrew when your opponent is moving to your left or when your hand is slightly to the outside (right) of the standard stance position, then you use the backfist in the opposite approach—when your hand is slightly to the left of its normal position or when your opponent is just to your right.

Unlike any other punch in JKD, the landing surface for the backfist is the back of the bottom three knuckles. It may be argued that the backfist is the fastest punch in JKD, for it lends itself to an easy whiplike motion, but you do not get as much power with it as you do with the pure straight. You just cannot generate as much force coming from this angle as you do shooting your hand straight out. Still, a fast, stinging backfist can certainly do damage.

Finger jabs are often incorporated into the backfist motion. This punch can also be combined with the straight lead by starting out with a backfist motion and then landing with the same surface area as you would a regular straight lead. (front as opposed to back of the bottom three knuckles). Footwork for the backfist is the same as for the regular straight lead. See Figures 108 through 110.

Figure 108: *The backfist from a modified JKD stance. Notice that the elbow points outward and is not tucked in close to the body as usual.*

Figure 109: *Hand shooting out for backfist.*

Figure 110: *The backfist at impact.*

SHOVEL HOOK

The shovel hook gives you an option to throw a low-line version of the straight. Its hooking relative is the uppercut. When you move into a crouch, usually accompanied by a slight weave to the right, you will be in position to throw a shovel hook. This is often where you come out of an evasive move, so the shovel hook makes a good counter. When you move out of the regular stance into a crouch and weave, your hand automatically turns over into a palms-up position. From there, you simply shoot out your lead hand with the palm up, again, landing with the bottom three knuckles. As with *all* JKD punches, you must rotate your hips so that your right hip points toward the target. To both facilitate and maximize rotation, the shovel hook is usually accompanied by a pivot step. Shovel hooks are especially useful for solar plexus and kidney shots. See Figures 111 through 114.

Figure 111: *Side view of shovel hook. The front hand is positioned so that extension of the arm makes this a linear, or straight, punch.*

Figure 112: *Side view of uppercut. Position of the hand in this case makes the uppercut a vertical punch, not a straight punch.*

Figure 113: *Front view of shovel hook, a variation of the straight lead, at impact.*

Figure 114: *Front view of uppercut, which is not a straight punch, at impact.*

THE DROP-SHIFT

Another low-line version of the straight, the drop-shift is a great way to remain unpredictable. You can shoot low with a drop-shift and then high or vice versa. The drop-shift is one of your safer offensive moves, since you can change both your height and angle. Your opponent will have a harder time countering. The drop-shift may be thrown with either hand. When thrown with the lead hand, you will have to turn your palm down. As with the corkscrew, this has to do with the angle and your power line. To execute a drop-shift, drop into a crouched position. This does not mean just your upper body. Bend at the knees. The lead hand drop-shift is usually accompanied by a side step the to the left or a pivot to the right. Again, you are able to alter both your height and angle, making you more elusive.[3] When facing a jabber, the drop-shift is a good countering option.[4] See Figures 115 and 116.

Figure 115: *Side view of the drop-shift.*

Figure 116: *The front view of the drop-shift.*

HAND POSITION

If you've studied any footage of Bruce Lee on film, then you know there was some variation in the way he held the lead hand. Again, to throw a pure straight, the fastest possible lead punch, we start from the stance—elbow bent, target within the gunsight. This gives us the least distance to travel to the target.

When we spar, however, we're dealing with different ranges, angles, punches, and combos. Lowering your hand can be used to bait your opponent into launching an attack that you can predict and then counter. Holding your front hand low also gives you more offensive options. You can mix it up to keep your opponent guessing. See Figures 102 and 117. According to Ted Wong, Bruce usually sparred with the lead hand held low:

> When we sparred, his hand was usually down. That's just the way he sparred. So relaxed. He was *fast*. Bruce Lee is Bruce Lee! He's going to be fast no matter where his hand is. The reason he held the hand down, though, was to draw you in. The front hand down is less threatening. It also gives you more choices. He said, "With the hand down, I can throw an uppercut. I can throw a hook. If your hand's up, you can only throw from that region." But if you really want to be fast, you go to the gun sight principle. It makes the distance shorter. Keeping the hand down also makes you more mobile. You're more balanced.[5]

Figure 117: *Variation of the JKD stance with low front hand.*

The next time you're sparring, I suggest that you try keeping your hand low for a little while. You'll have to be extra precise in your judgment of distance to avoid being hit. And keep that left hand up! But you should notice (1) much greater mobility and (2) that you have so many more options. You can set up a pattern of hooking high and then suddenly uppercut from below. Or set up a pattern of straight leads and then suddenly hook. Also see if your opponent is more likely to attack when your hand is low, giving you more opportunities to attack by drawing.

As I'll discuss in Chapter Eleven, you can see this variation of the stance in action if you go to Bruce's films.

NOTES

[1] Jack Dempsey, *Championship Fighting: Explosive Punching and Aggressive Defence* (New York: Prentice Hall, Inc., 1950), pp. 97–98. It's likely the term "pivot step" came from Dempsey. Here, he describes its use with the corkscrew hook: "You'll step in most with the left corkscrew. But when you stop with the corkscrew, you do not move in with the straight-forward falling step. Instead, you move in with a 'pivot step.'"

[2] Ibid., p. 71.

[3] Bruce Lee, ed. John Little, *Jeet Kune Do: Bruce Lee's Commentaries on the Martial Way* (Boston: Tuttle Publishing, 1997), p. 196.

[4] Edwin L. Haislet, *Boxing* (New York: A.S. Barnes & Noble Company, 1940), p. 23. See for excellent illustrations of the drop-shift.

[5] In conversation with Ted Wong, June 8, 2004.

WHAT JUN FAN JEET KUNE DO IS NOT—IT'S NOT KALI, ESCRIMA, OR 27 ARTS

For over thirty years now, certain so-called JKD instructors have been teaching techniques that were never developed or practiced by Bruce Lee. In some cases, they have taken certain arts—Southeast Asian arts like kali and escrima, for example—and misrepresented them as JKD. This is disrespectful not only to Bruce Lee but also to masters of these other arts. *Nowhere* in Bruce Lee's writings will you find notes on kali or escrima techniques. In fact, nowhere in Bruce Lee's private notes will you find an in-depth analysis of any arts other than Western fencing and boxing, and in earlier years, Wing Chun.[1]

JKD is not kali. It is not escrima. And it is most certainly *not*, as some so-called JKD instructors have described it, a cluttered mess of "27 arts." No proof for this claim can be found in any of Bruce Lee's published or private notes. If he only briefly mentioned other arts, it was to understand their strengths and shortcomings, so that he could find ways to defeat them. In an actual fight, there is no time to "flow" in and out of 27 different arts. There is no such thing as "JKD blend," as it is sometimes called.

Basing all the techniques of a single system on the same principles of boxing and fencing, the laws of physics, and the mechanics of the human body, is quite different from haphazardly collecting techniques from a dozen other arts. It is doubtful that the creators of a "style" that borrows from so many other arts have investigated each technique sufficiently to prove their scientific validity. Their instruction is often a long litany of, "First you do this, *and then* you do this *and then* you do this, *and then* you do this." And as Bruce himself said,

"While you are remembering all the '*and thens*' the other guy is killing you"[2]—probably with the straight lead. Again, in Bruce Lee's writings, the only techniques given enough consideration for actual application and incorporation into JKD come from the same three arts—fencing, boxing, and, though eventually discarded, Wing Chun.

IT'S NOT WING CHUN

JKD is *not* a modified version of Wing Chun as some have misrepresented it. As I've discussed throughout this book, the inadequacies of the traditional arts are what forced Bruce to adopt the principles of Western fencing and boxing in the first place. Yes, he initially studied Wing Chun. And, yes, he wrote about and practiced it. But remember, this was early in his development as a fighter. As anyone who's seen backyard training footage of Bruce knows, by the late 1960s, he'd traded in his Wing Chun dummy for the heavy bag.

In a letter to William Cheung that we've already referred to, Bruce had stopped practicing Wing Chun by 1967. While much of Bruce's research on traditional martial arts in the early 1960s has been published, anything he wrote after 1967 should be considered JKD research. Some Wing Chun instructors like to claim that Wing Chun is the foundation of Jeet Kune Do and that Bruce Lee merely expanded on it. *Wrong*. He had all but *abandoned* it. Its shortcomings are what forced him to look for a completely different way of fighting. It's difficult to comprehend where this misunderstanding originates, because it is so clearly documented in Bruce Lee's letter to Cheung. How much more clearly can you say, as Bruce does in the letter, "I've lost faith in the Chinese classical arts"? He goes on to say the "reason for my not sticking to Wing Chun [is] because I sincerely feel that this style [JKD] has more to offer regarding efficiency."[3, 4]

WESTERN STRUCTURE

So, from a technical point of view, let's take a look at some of that JKD efficiency. Structurally, the stance and mechanics of JKD are completely different. As shown in Figure 118, the traditional stance is a very open, squared off stance. The JKD stance, much like a fencer's stance is more closed and closes even further when the lead punch is thrown, providing further protection of the centerline. The open stance, on the other hand, remains just as open at rest as it does when a punch is thrown.

The stance and mechanics of the straight lead also provide greater reach to your opponent and, in many cases, will allow you to hit without being hit. A more open stance does not allow for hip rotation and restricts reach. On the other hand, the hip rotation and shoulder extension of the JKD straight lead puts non-JKD practitioners within your striking range. And even against opponents who are much taller with greater arm length, you will still be out of their reach.

Figure 118: *As you can see, the structure of the JKD straight lead (right) is entirely different from that of the traditional, open-stance punch (left). Even though your opponent may have a greater wingspan, the structure of the JKD stance and the mechanics of the punch may still allow you to reach your opponent while he or she is unable to reach you.*

FOOTWORK

Perhaps the most glaring difference between JKD and Wing Chun is in the footwork of each system. Wing Chun is almost purely linear in its movement. There's forward and back, turn to the left, turn to the right. That's it. On the other hand, as discussed earlier, JKD has the pivoting, curving step that allows a fighter to cover distance and change angles simultaneously. This opens up a vastly greater range of angles, much like those employed by boxers at close range.[5]

Timing-wise, Wing Chun is, like most Eastern arts, a whole-beat art. The footwork does not allow for direction change or other movement on the half-beat. With its heavy fencing influence, JKD, on the other hand, allows for attack or evasion at *any* time. We've only touched on the footwork possibilities in this volume. Again, the footwork that is the foundation of JKD could be the subject of an entire book itself. Suffice to say that you should be able to fire a shot at any time—whole beat or half-beat—from any angle, no matter where your weight is distributed—on the front foot, the back foot, in the air. True Jun Fan Jeet Kune Do footwork allows for this.

IT'S NOT BOXING

While Bruce may have discarded Wing Chun for the western arts of fencing and boxing, Jeet Kune Do is not a simplified version of those arts either. To the untrained eye, it may appear as though Jeet Kune Do is nothing more than a fancy name for boxing or kickboxing. This is a common misconception not helped by the fact that, for years, certain people have been teaching what is essentially boxing and passing it off as JKD. So, let's review a few points to clarify.

STRONG SIDE FORWARD

Although Bruce took many of the technical nuances of the straight lead from Dempsey and Driscoll, remember that in JKD, we place the strong hand (the right hand for most people) in front. The stance is constructed for optimal delivery of the lead punch. The set up for boxing is the reverse. The boxing stance is constructed around delivery of the rear hand. While the left jab is used to set up the right cross in boxing, the boxing stance is designed for optimal delivery of the rear hand.

When Tuttle Publishing released its volumes of the Bruce Lee Library in the late 1990s, there was quite a bit of confusion. Students learning from supposed JKD practitioners had been taught to fight in boxing stances with the left, or weaker side, in front. What they were reading in Bruce Lee's own words was contradictory. A whole lot of head scratching and backpedaling followed.

Just a side note here—if you are looking for a Jeet Kune Do instructor, there are certain fundamental elements that must be in place. Chief among these elements is that the strong hand be in front. Even if the instructor knows nothing else, any JKD practitioner should at least have the strong hand as the lead. If the instructor doesn't know this, he or she is not only unfamiliar with the most basic aspects of JKD but also obviously hasn't even bothered to read Bruce Lee.

THE STANCE

The long-range JKD stance from which you will deliver the straight lead is also different from boxing in its foot placement. In an orthodox boxing stance, even though one foot is still in front of the other, your shoulders are squared off to your opponent. Even in the more modern boxing stance, you are still more squared off than in the JKD on-guard. In the modern boxing stance your front toe is aligned with the heel of your rear foot. Remember in the JKD stance, your front toe is aligned with the *arch* of your rear foot.

This difference serves to narrow your target area. It is much more of a fencer's stance. When you go to deliver the straight lead, the area you reveal to your opponent as a target actually diminishes. You are both more defensive and offensive at the same time. In boxing, on the other hand, nothing changes as you throw the front hand, because the boxing jab does not have foot placement that allows for that extra turn of the hip that would make you a narrower target. At the end of the boxing jab, you remain facing your opponent as squarely as when you started.

Remember from our experiment at the end of the stance chapter that the alignment of the JKD lead punch was designed to best absorb impact of the equal and opposite force exerted by the target. Also remember from this experiment that the boxing jab was not as effective in absorbing those forces.

There are times, of course, when you will have to engage in in-fighting that will require you to square off a bit more to allow for better leverage at close range. And at this range, you will cease to throw pure straight leads.

But the whole idea of being able to throw the JKD lead is that it gives you added range. In a fight, you want to hit and *not* get hit. Straight punching makes this possible.

THUMBS UP

True, you might call this element of the straight lead a vestige of old timey boxing. Bruce drew from the boxing literature before his time. Dempsey, Driscoll, and Haislet all threw their lead hands thumbs up. Recall the reason for this is what Dempsey called the power line. It is a much more stable punch that sends more force in your opponent's direction and puts you at less risk for hand and wrist injuries. While this JKD element comes from early-twentieth-century boxing, it is something you almost never see today.

GREATER RANGE

Part of what gives the Jeet Kune Do lead a unique advantage over other arts is that it affords crucial inches of additional striking range. As you can see from Figure 119, the structure of the stance and the hip-turn mechanics enable you to cover precious extra distance. This is what Driscoll meant when he titled one of his boxing textbooks *Outfighting or Long Range*

Boxing.[6] How reassuring it is to know that against a non-JKD practitioner, or an incorrectly trained one, that you can hit at will without worrying about being hit yourself?.

Figure 119: *The stance and mechanics of the JKD straight lead allow for greater range than the stance and mechanics of the boxing jab. Even with my shorter wingspan, I am still able to reach my opponent with the JKD lead, while he is unable to reach me with a boxing jab.*

THE FENCING CONNECTION

Jeet Kune Do may look a bit like boxing simply because we throw punches and wear boxing gear when we spar, but of the two Western influences on JKD, fencing is actually the more prevalent. It is most likely that Bruce Lee first researched boxing literature from earlier decades when it seemed to be common knowledge that English boxing had evolved out of fencing. As we've seen, both Haislet and Driscoll drew many parallels to fencing—the straight thrust, the stop-hit, the fighting measure.[7]

It is from this boxing literature, that Bruce probably got the idea to delve into fencing and the work of Nadi, Castello, Martinez, and Crosnier.[8] So many of the strategic variables in JKD come from fencing. Cadence, broken rhythm, the fencing measure. The name "Jeet Kune Do" itself, is essentially another way of saying "stop-hit."

So, if anyone tells you JKD is merely boxing, correct him or her and explain that it is really fencing. Or as Bruce said, "It is Western sword fencing—without the sword."[9]

EVIDENCE ON FILM

As I'll discuss in the next chapter, the easiest way to settle these issues is to see for yourself. Watch Bruce on film—either in his theatrical releases or private training and sparring footage—and you'll see that unlike boxers, he places the strong side, his right side, in front. When he throws a straight lead, it's with the thumb up, not palm down. Look at his stance. Have you ever seen Bruce in a closed Wing Chun stance like that? No, a Wing Chun stance is open and squared off. Look at Bruce's footwork. Do you see Wing Chun practitioners with the same bounce and spring of boxers and fencers? Of course, not. In sparring footage especially, do you see Bruce "flowing" in and out of different styles? No, he's mostly throwing straight leads, stop-hits, and front-leg kicks. That's it. It's a few simple techniques applied to perfection with regard to mechanics, timing, and distance.[10] I've laid out the published evidence for you here, but as always, the best evidence is Bruce himself.

NOTES

[1] You will not find a single mention of kali or escrima in any of Bruce Lee's published notes. You will not find any analysis or investigation of either art in *The Tao of Jeet Kune Do*, the six volumes of Tuttle's *Bruce Lee Library*, nor the *Fighting Method* series. And in my own research for this book, having had access to some of Lee's notes, I found not one reference to these Southeastern arts.

[2] Bruce Lee, ed. John Little, *Jeet Kune Do: Bruce Lee's Commentaries on the Martial Way* (Boston: Tuttle Publishing, 1997), p. 38.

[3] Lee, ed. John Little, *Letters of the Dragon: Correspondence, 1958–1973*, (Boston: Tuttle Publishing, 1998), pp. 110–111.

[4] Ibid, p. 124. In a letter to Wong Shun-Leung, Bruce seems to be hinting at the superiority of Western boxing over Wing Chun, stating that he often practices with boxers and says, "There are many so-called masters in Wing Chun here, I really hope that they will not be so blind [as] to fight with those Western boxers!"

[5] Ibid, p. 33. John Little notes the lack of "curved" movements in Wing Chun.

[6] Jim Driscoll, *Outfighting or Long Ranging Boxing*, (London: Athletic Publications, LTD.). An excellent 76-page explanation of all the advantages of long-range boxing.

[7] Captain John Godfrey ed. W. C. Heinz, "The Useful Science of Defence" in *The Fireside Book of Boxing* (New York: Simon and Schuster, 1961), pp. 158–162.
You'll see this book on Bruce Lee's bookshelf—along with Dempsey and Haislet—in the

documentary *Bruce Lee: A Warrior's Journey*. Published in 1747, Godfrey's book was the first to give credit for the development of boxing to fencing.

[8] In conversation with Ted Wong, June 8, 2004

[9] Bruce Lee, ed. John Little, *Jeet Kune Do: Bruce Lee's Commentaries on the Martial Way* (Boston: Tuttle Publishing, 1997), p. 210. Again, compare with Driscoll, *The Straight Lead and How to Cultivate It* (London: Athletic Publications, Ltd.), p. 27: "It is practically sword fencing without a sword, and follows in all its movements, or, rather, should follow, the same principles."

[10] As we'll discuss in the next chapter, you can see these things for yourself in *Bruce Lee: A Warrior's Journey* at about the 21-minute mark.

GO TO THE SOURCE

Before we conclude our exploration of the straight lead, let's remember that everything Jeet Kune Do begins and ends with Bruce Lee. Everything presented in this book has its origins in Bruce's writings—and their original sources—as well as instruction from Ted Wong, who has shared much of the firsthand instruction he received from Bruce.

Over the years, certain individuals have used the name Jeet Kune Do to promote themselves, other arts, and techniques that have no foundation in Bruce Lee's work—or basic laws of science, for that matter. To make things easy, though, it's not a matter of "he said, she said." It's a matter of *science*. I hope that the arguments presented in this book have at least shed some light on why Bruce Lee made the technical choices that he did. Again, he didn't throw just anything into the mix. After years of researching fighting science, he chose the thumbs-up, strong-side-forward lead punch. He didn't throw in the left-handed, palm-down boxing jab, too, just because he could. He made a conscious choice to include certain elements, to the exclusion of others. These are scientifically based choices.

If people choose to add to their martial arts repertoire, fine. If their additions are true improvements, even better. But they should not misrepresent those elements as Jeet Kune Do. Otherwise, it becomes impossible to know what elements truly came from Bruce Lee. And if those added, non-JKD elements have proven to be so effective, why not take credit for it? Why hide under the name of Jeet Kune Do? Those who have practiced other disciplines or their own inventions but called it Jeet Kune Do all these years have slowly eroded Bruce Lee's art. It's time to reclaim it.

This will take some time, because there's a lot of stuff out there masquerading as Jeet Kune Do. There's an easy way around this, though, and all it takes is a little common sense. Go to the source.

SEE BRUCE MOVE

There are limitations to the written word and still pictures. I could talk at you all day, but a book alone is not going to get you a perfect straight lead. I can describe some things that you might not be able to figure out on your own from observation, and scientific explanations should increase your understanding of what's happening—and, more important, *why*—when you throw the lead punch. But as Bruce said, "The essence of fighting is the art of moving."[1] You've got to know what the lead punch looks like in motion.

The best thing you can do when trying to differentiate the imposters from the real thing is to watch the real thing. Watch Bruce. So, let's go over some accessible examples of Bruce on film demonstrating the straight lead. One word of caution before we get started: the man was fast! I recommend taking the remote to your DVD player and watching these scenes frame by frame to fully appreciate Bruce's artistry. I've included the times at which these scenes occur, but be aware that as DVDs are reissued or released in other countries, the time codes vary slightly.

BRUCE LEE: A WARRIOR'S JOURNEY

1-INCH PUNCH

Based on what we know about the straight lead and Jeet Kune Do's underlying themes of efficiency and economy of motion, it's not surprising that some of the best visual examples can be found, not in Bruce Lee's films, but in the documentary *Bruce Lee: A Warrior's Journey*. The few seconds of home and demonstration footage give us an idea of what JKD looks like in a form less staged for film.

At 29 minutes and 35 seconds into the DVD, you'll see Bruce demonstrate his famous 1-inch punch at the 1967 International Karate Tournament. While it is not exactly the standard lead punch we have discussed throughout much of this book, the 1-inch punch is the straight in microcosm, essentially the straight lead at the point of impact. It demonstrates how construction of the stance and proper mechanics give us maximum leverage and force production at the point of impact without the benefit of wind-up or momentum.

The hand is positioned 1 inch away from the target. Notice how Bruce's arm is bent just enough to allow for about 3 inches to punch through the target. Remember, this is where a pushing motion would have the greatest leverage. Bruce goes through the motions of hip rotation. Prior to the actual punch, you'll see him hunker down a little, giving him the "small phasic bent knee" discussed earlier. Again, that bent knee gives him room from which to push. If his legs were already straightened, he'd have nowhere left to go, and because he is not covering any distance with his feet, he'll need the extra vertical force, or ground reaction force, to generate power. The position of his legs and feet just prior to delivering the punch is exactly where yours would be before pushing off for a regular straight lead.

You probably wouldn't expect too much footwork from a punch delivered from only 1 inch away, but look closely. As he settles down before striking, you'll see his left heel come up. As his hips rotate, you'll see him transfer his weight, changing from a 50-50 distribution on both feet to placing more of his weight in the front leg. The left foot pushes off the ground. His fist hits the target. The right foot readjusts, coming slightly off the ground to accommodate for the weight transfer. The rear foot lands. Voilà. A push-off and three-point landing, all in place. The lesson here is that every punch in Jeet Kune Do requires footwork, even if you're not covering distance.

Also notice that Bruce's center of gravity never overtakes his front leg. Even though he is transferring his weight forward to the front foot, his center of gravity never falls outside the base determined by his foot position. This is how balance is maintained.

THE STRAIGHT BLAST

At the 29 minute and 8 second mark, you'll find a variation of the straight lead in the straight blast, which is a succession of straight right and left hand blows. In this case, Bruce is throwing a straight blast at the heavy bag. The punch is delivered from a low line, making it very close to being a shovel hook. What I want you to notice in this example is the weight transfer. All three directions of force are accounted for here. There is rotation at the hips. With each punch, he is also pushing off with tremendous ground reaction force. Finally, he is sending his weight toward the bag by hitting through it.

RESOURCES

At 20 min 13 sec, we get a peek at Bruce's own copies of Roger Crosnier and Edwin Haislet's books, with Bruce's meticulous notes written in them. And at 31 minutes and 8 seconds, we see *The Fireside Book of Boxing*, which as you may recall contains an excerpt from Captain Godfrey's book, the first publication to credit fencing for the resurgence of British boxing.

THE STOP-HIT

I've saved the best for last. Two perfect examples of the straight lead applied to a combative situation. The first can be seen at the 21 minutes and 16 seconds mark. It's the 1967 International Karate Tournament, and Bruce is sparring. First, notice how incredibly relaxed Bruce is and the variation in position of his lead hand. Most of the time it is left down at his side. In this first example, as his opponent rushes in on him, Bruce uses two of the simplest forms of offensive defense. First, he throws out a front leg obstruction to counter a kick, and then he shoots a straight lead to his opponent's head.[2] The timing and distance had to be perfect to pull off these counters.

This is about as simple and utterly unglamorous as it gets. There is absolutely nothing flashy about these counters. As soon as his opponent so much as twitches, he's thrown out that lead hand as straight as can be. If you blink, you'll miss it. Compare this to the more exaggerated and busier movements of Bruce in his films. This is one I really suggest you freeze and then watch frame by frame.

A few seconds later at the 21 minutes and 23 seconds point, we get another great example of the stop-hit. Before his opponent can even get his kick off the ground, Bam! Bruce has already popped him with the straight lead. Remember, the hand and arm will always move faster than the foot and leg.

This is a great example of the importance of footwork. Bruce uses the step and slide, and small, controlled push-offs to maintain the fighting measure. He backs up once with a step and slide—one whole beat. This sets his opponent up for what follows. Bruce completes the first half of another step backward, but on the half-beat, he reverses direction and tags his opponent again. So, here we have the maintenance of distance, timing, and the set up all achieved through footwork.

Just as Driscoll observed with most straight leads, it doesn't even seem as if Bruce throws a very hard punch here. He doesn't need to. His opponent's own weight and momentum works against him once he runs into the stop-hit. A correctly timed stop-hit should be almost effortless.

Again, pretty simple stuff. Bruce's opponent may never have seen the punch coming, and it all happens so quickly on film. Have that remote ready for frame-by-frame viewing. Perhaps this is why we don't have a textbook example of the pure straight lead in a Bruce Lee film. It's not the easiest thing for the untrained eye to perceive. In film, you want the audience to see the action. In a real fight, you want your opponent never to know what hit him.

ENTER THE DRAGON

BACKFIST VARIATION

The martial arts in *Enter the Dragon* are quite a bit more theatrical than what Bruce would use for sparring, or what I'd call Backyard JKD, but there are still a couple of really good examples here. Bruce faces off in the tournament with Bob Wall. This scene appears at 61 minutes and 35 seconds into the film.

The punch really is too fast to see, let alone fully appreciate. Slow it down and you'll see the mechanics that make it so incredibly fast. First, this is a backfist, not a pure straight lead. Remember, the backfist, though lacking the power of a standard straight, is the fastest punch in JKD. And some of that lost power can be compensated for by speed because force equals mass times acceleration. As a backfist, the hand starts to the left (Bruce's left) of the center line, whips out, and then returns to the left of the center line. And if you really look closely, you'll see what he's actually throwing is a finger jab.

Aside from the trajectory of the hand, though, everything else about this punch is exactly the same as it would be for a pure straight lead. The hand moves ever so slightly before the feet. What follows is a beautiful example of the push-off and the three-point landing. Bruce launches off the left leg. He smacks Bob Wall's face. That's landing number one. The right foot lands on the ground. That's two. The left foot hits the ground. Three. As we've learned from Dempsey, you redirect the downward gravitational force of your body hurtling toward the ground by hitting the target before the front foot lands. That way, most of your body weight goes toward the target and not into the ground.

The second example occurs at 61 minutes and 50 seconds, giving us another angle, a different look, at the same punch.

I'd like to emphasize the textbook illustration of the push-off here, especially in the first example. Note the depth, power, and incredible explosiveness. I don't know if Bruce was trying to make a statement here, but by placing the two characters in a Wing Chun set up with their two forearms touching, he certainly showed the effectiveness of a JKD straight punch over traditional arts. No other art has a punch like this, and the footwork, its sheer power and speed, is what sets the JKD straight lead apart.

THE SET UP

In his final showdown with Han (Shih Kien) at the 93 minutes and 27 seconds mark, there's a great example of how to use the lead hand for set ups. Having already been peppered by Bruce's lead kicks, Han is ripe for flinching. Bruce feints high with the lead hand, then fakes low, again with the front hand. Han, poor sap, falls for both, leaving him a sitting duck for getting a sidekick in the ear. And then Bruce really gets mad. WRRRAAAAAAGH!

RETURN OF THE DRAGON

According to Ted Wong, *Return of the Dragon* has more JKD elements than any other Bruce Lee film:

> Oh, he was very excited because that was the movie that he was really proud of. He had written it, he had directed it, and he was the star of it. It was his baby. I think that movie had more JKD in it than any other movie he did. It really represented his thinking, his way of martial art.[3]

The final showdown in this film with Chuck Norris in the Coliseum does have it all—footwork, stop-hits, setup's, broken rhythm, you name it. Let's start with the footwork. At the beginning of the fight (83 minutes and 30 seconds into the film),[4] Bruce avoids Chuck's kick with a pendulum step. Then at 84 minutes and 51 seconds, there's a fantastic slow-mo sequence. You'll see Bruce pivoting, circling, circling left. Notice the small steps. Then at 85 minutes and 3 seconds, he pivots right. We've only touched on the most basic footwork in this book, but notice the pivoting with the bouncing and half-beat footwork. All of this keeps Bruce mobile, always in balance, and ready to seize any striking opportunity. There are also great examples of coordination between the upper and lower body. Again, beyond the scope of this book, but these are great defensive moves.

However great these examples are, though, you can see the difference between this staged fight and the footage of Bruce actually sparring in *Bruce Lee: A Warrior's Journey*. As Ted Wong notes, when sparring, Bruce was actually quite still. He didn't bounce around nearly as much as he does in this film and only did so when the situation called for it.[5]

Moving on, let's look at an example of the straight as a counterattack. Chuck throws a punch. Bruce slips and parries. Chuck throws another punch. Bruce pulls back and then on the half-beat, reverses direction and counters with a straight lead. It's a shame that you can't see Bruce's feet in this shot. His hand, as usual, is held low and as relaxed as can be before whipping out a greased lightning straight.

This entire fight at the end of *Return of the Dragon* certainly is the best movie representation of Jeet Kune Do tactics. We're only going to talk about how they relate to the straight lead, but know there's a heckuva lot going on here with kicks and other weapons as well. At 86 minutes and 27 seconds, we have a fantastic example of a set up using the straight lead. Having already established the threat of the lead hand in the counterattack example just discussed, Bruce is free to use the straight punch for progressive indirect attacks. He feints high. Chuck's character flails high. Bruce then goes low. At 86 minutes and 33 seconds, Bruce repeats the same scenario. He feints high, then fakes low. He's establishing a pattern, attempting to lull Chuck into a motor-set mode. Notice that in both instances, Bruce has his hand low. The feints and fakes start with his hand in this low position. After two repetitions, Chuck's character expects more of the same and never sees that high hook that thwacks him on the side of the head. This is the beauty of keeping the front hand low. You can throw uppercuts, high hooks, low hooks, shovel hooks, corkscrews, and, of course, the straight lead from this position. It's much more deceptive than keeping both hands up all the time.

Finally, at 86 minutes and 55 seconds, we have a textbook example of the stop hit. But first we must set a pattern. Chuck kicks. Bruce backs away. Chuck kicks again. Bruce backs away. Chuck starts to kick once more. Third time's a charm. On the half-beat, Bruce moves in to intercept with the straight then follows with a cross, a hook, another cross, and another hook. Not pretty. It's all down hill for Chuck's character after that.

OTHER SOURCES

If you want to see someone in the flesh properly executing Jeet Kune Do techniques, I'd recommend the man who spent more time than anyone else in private instruction with Bruce himself, Ted Wong.[6] If you can, attend one of his seminars. If not, there are some good video sources. Though difficult to obtain, taped segments from the annual Bruce Lee seminars held by the Jun Fan Jeet Kune Do Nucleus in the late 1990s were made available for a limited time. There's also a video produced by *Black Belt Magazine* featuring Ted Wong and Richard Bustillo. There isn't much explanation of the straight lead, but you can at least observe Ted Wong's technique, his stance, and footwork, all of which are consistent with the teachings and writings of Bruce Lee.

Finally, at the 2003 Bruce Lee convention in Burbank, some footage of Bruce sparring was shown. At the time of this writing, plans are under way to eventually release this footage in which Bruce lands straight lead after straight lead. Perhaps by the time this book is published, it will be available to the public.

PROPER INSTRUCTION

It always amazes me that people pay good money to learn Jeet Kune Do from instructors who supposedly teach Bruce Lee's art but move *nothing* like Bruce. That's fine if you like what you're learning, but if you want to throw a straight lead, then you'd be better off with repeated viewings of the clips I've just mentioned. I'm not saying you have to find someone who moves exactly like Bruce. But there are some fundamental elements that should be there, things we've outlined in this book that can be found in Bruce Lee's own writings—the strong side forward, proper alignment, thumbs-up lead hand, snappy follow-through, correct movement sequence, an explosive push-off, and light and precise footwork.

Finally, if you're going to learn something from someone, doesn't it make sense that he be able to perform the technique he's trying to teach? Again, sounds like common sense, but you'd be surprised. Before you follow anyone's instruction, you need to see for yourself. Can this person hit? Move? Even better, hold the focus pads for the instructor. You should feel accuracy and focused, explosive force in every punch. It would also make sense that he spar. For how else could the instructor know how to apply the techniques he is trying to teach you?

If you're still not sure, go back to the clips I've just discussed. Even if you're on the right track with a good instructor, you should still be spending hours with those clips, with Bruce. Watch them. Analyze them. Remember them. The answers are there.

NOTES

[1] Lee, *Tao of Jeet Kune Do,* p. 143.

[2] As Bruce mentioned on the show *Longstreet,* he uses his longest weapon, the sidekick, against the nearest target, his opponent's kneecap.

[3] Ted Wong with John Little, "An Interview with Ted Wong," *Bruce Lee: The Official Publication & Voice of the Jun Fan Jeet Kune Do Nucleus,* February 1998, p. 12. Also in conversation with Ted Wong March, 18, 2004,

[4] The DVD for this analysis is from the *Bruce Lee Thirtieth Anniversary Commemorative Edition* released in the UK and in Region 2 format. Time counters may vary from region to region.

[5] In conversation with Ted Wong, March 18, 2004.

[6] Once again, for a list of Wong's Jeet Kune Do credentials see the interview in this book.

BACK TO THE ROOTS

We began with the roots of Jeet Kune Do, so it makes sense that we should return to those roots as our look at the straight lead draws to a close. "What we are after in JKD," according to Bruce Lee, "is the *root* and not the branches. The root is the real knowledge; the branches are surface knowledge. Real knowledge breeds 'body feel' and personal expression. Surface knowledge breeds mechanical conditioning, imposes limitations, and squelches creativity."[1]

Over the years, some have misinterpreted Bruce's words regarding personal expression to mean "anything goes"—that by taking a little bit of this and a little bit of that from many different arts means they are practicing JKD. Ironically, this leads to the very surface knowledge and mechanical conditioning that Bruce was railing against. Jeet Kune Do is not the pointless accumulation of knowledge. Simply taking elements from other arts and placing them outside the context of their original systems is not only illogical. It's also disrespectful. Bastardizing other arts with no rhyme or reason leads to the most surface and shallow levels of understanding. Does the perpetrator know the underlying mechanics and principles behind a pilfered technique? Does he know how to *use* it in a combative situation?

True understanding means knowing a particular technique from all angles—all the advantages, all the disadvantages, when and when not to use it. It means knowing that technique inside and out and being able to explain the whys behind the biomechanics. A technique should not be incorporated into any system until these questions have been answered.

X AND Y

Remember, Bruce did not choose everything for his fighting system. He chose certain things—the thumbs-up fist, the raised heel, the rapier—to the exclusion of others—the palm-down fist, the grounded heel, and the broadsword. We have spent much of this book explaining Bruce's reasoning behind his choices.

Boxing has been called the sweet science, and if JKD is a science as well—and it is—then there are certain laws of science that must be followed. These are not just strategic, fighting science laws, but laws of physics, the effects of which we experience every day. These are rules of gravity and motion that govern the physical world in which we live.

While Bruce may have said Jeet Kune Do is "only a name," make no mistake. It *is* its own system. To practice something else and still call it Jeet Kune Do, to misrepresent Jeet Kune Do, is to deny its very existence. Whether committed out of malice or ignorance, to do so desecrates Bruce Lee's name.

For those of you who are still not convinced, you need only turn to page 50 of *Bruce Lee's Commentaries on the Martial Way*:

- X is Jeet Kune Do.
- Y is the style you will represent.
- To represent and teach Y one should drill its members according to the preaching of Y.
- This is the same with anyone who is qualified and has been approved to represent X.
- To justify by interfusing X and Y is basically the denying of Y—but still calling it Y.
- A man, as you put it, is one who is noble to stick to the road he has chosen.
- A garden of roses will yield roses, and a garden of violets will yield violets.[2]

For many years now, people have been practicing Y and calling it X. The purpose of this book has been to shed a little light on what X really is. The tale of X and Y, by the way, is taken from a letter from Bruce to his student Jerry Poteet, who wanted to mix JKD drills with kenpo karate. Obviously Bruce objected.[3]

The strongest evidence against the idea that JKD is anything you want it to be comes from Bruce himself:

In any physical movement *there is always a most efficient and alive manner to accomplish the purpose of the performance* for each individual. That is, in regard to proper leverage, balance in movement, economical and efficient use of motion and energy, etc. Live, efficient movement that liberates is one thing; sterile classical sets that bind and condition is another.[4]

There is a crucial distinction here. It is one thing to follow the laws of science. It is quite another to blindly follow what is popular "knowledge." We used to think the earth was flat, but it has since been scientifically proven that it is not. That doesn't mean we now revert to declaring that it's flat just because we feel like it.

The same should apply to JKD. We used to think throwing a jab one way was effective. Over thousands of years of evolution and with Bruce Lee's research, we were introduced to a much more effective fighting system and a better way to throw a punch. Unfortunately, instead of building on and refining what Bruce Lee developed, there are those who say— again, whether out of malice or ignorance—that adding untested and unrelated techniques or technical embellishments means they are improving JKD. Wrong.

What they are doing is anti-JKD in two ways. First, they are deviating from the very scientific, physical laws on which the art was built. Two, adding techniques is also philosophically anti-JKD, for as Bruce himself wrote, "It is not how much one learns but how much one has absorbed in what he has learned. The best techniques are the simple ones, executed correctly."[5] Once again, go back to the roots.

And of his students, Bruce said, "[They] will realize the futile search for more and more new techniques. Rather they will devote the needed hours to practicing the correct execution of simple techniques."[6] Unfortunately, this has not always been the case. Instead of spending the required time on refining and perfecting the fundamentals—stance, mechanics, footwork—so-called JKD practitioners skip steps, add to techniques without investigating, and never ever grasp the most fundamental principles on which the art was built. Worst still, they misrepresent their mish-mash as JKD.

If someone wants to add a technique to his arsenal or embellish on an existing JKD technique, fine. But do *not* call it Jeet Kune Do. And he should be prepared to back up the validity of its use with sound, scientific evidence.

Publicly, he may have said he didn't believe in styles, but Bruce Lee clearly saw JKD as something that stands apart from other systems. "My JKD," he wrote in a letter to a friend, "is really something else . . . more and more I pity the martial arts that are blinded by their partiality and ignorance."[7]

"HAVING NO FORM" VERSUS HAVING "NO-FORM"

Over the years, many have misinterpreted Bruce Lee's words regarding "no way as way." They practice and teach whatever they want and then call it Jeet Kune Do, and as a result, the actual techniques that Bruce Lee developed are being lost.

Remember, Bruce was questioning thousands of years of classical martial arts training. We need to place his words in their proper context. At that time, he realized classical arts had not progressed and that their techniques were based on tradition, not science.

Today, however, the pendulum has swung too far in the opposite direction. Much of what masquerades as JKD is undisciplined, unscientific, and utterly disorganized chaos. It seems that Bruce did, in fact, anticipate this misconception when he wrote the following:

> People often mistakenly [believe] that JKD is against form. I don't think I'll go into detail on that, as other paragraphs will clarify that. One thing we must understand: that is, there is always a most efficient and alive manner to carry out a movement (and that the basic laws of leverage, body position, balance, foot-work, and so forth, are not to be violated). However, alive, efficient form is one thing; sterile classical sets that bind and condition are another. Aside from the above mentioned, one must also distinguish the subtlety between "having no form" and having "no-form." The first is ignorance, the second transcendence.[8]

There is a crucial distinction being drawn here. As stated above, the "basic laws," the laws of science are "not to be violated." *Not to be violated.* Failure to master the basics is what Bruce referred to as "having no form." This is simply ignorance.

"No-form," in contrast, is that level of skill at which the basics have been mastered to the degree that their use is purely instinctual. This doesn't mean that there isn't a correct way of doing things. Obviously, from the passage above, Bruce believed there are right and wrong ways of performing techniques. "No-form" is that level of executing those techniques to such perfection that doing so no longer requires thought.[9] This is transcendence, but it can only be reached once the basics have been honed and perfected.

JUN FAN JEET KUNE DO VERSUS JEET KUNE DO

Now would be a good time to address the title of this book, which uses the term *Jun Fan Jeet Kune Do* instead of Jeet Kune Do. Because of Bruce Lee's unexpected death, ownership of the name Jeet Kune Do was never claimed, and those who have since capitalized on this situation have nearly destroyed his art. Tragically, they have rendered the name Jeet Kune Do meaningless.

True, Bruce Lee believed in progression and improvement, but the confusion and misrepresentation of JKD over the last three decades has made it impossible for future generations to determine what information actually originated from Bruce Lee himself.

After much legal work, the Bruce Lee Foundation has reclaimed the name Jun Fan Jeet Kune Do to represent the authentic teachings of Bruce Lee. "Jun Fan," Lee's Chinese name, has been added to the original name Jeet Kune Do to differentiate between Bruce Lee's art and that of those who would misrepresent it.

The purpose of this book has been to set the record straight, not only by referring to Lee's own writings, but also by going one step further and tracing those sources that had influenced him. In the service of brevity, we've used the original term Jeet Kune Do, but the material presented throughout this volume, as indicated by the title, does fall under the name Jun Fan Jeet Kune Do.

Designation of specific instructional material as Jun Fan Jeet Kune Do must be approved by the Bruce Lee Foundation. For more information on the name Jun Fan Jeet Kune Do and where to find accurate instruction and information on the art of Jun Fan Jeet Kune Do, visit the official site of the Bruce Lee Foundation at www.bruceleefoundation.com.

PHYSICAL WORLD

All of the confusion and controversy surrounding JKD today, of course, stems from the fact that Bruce Lee's untimely death meant that we were never left with a definitive textbook on the most advanced stages of JKD. The notes that became the *Tao of Jeet Kune Do* and *Bruce Lee's Commentaries on the Martial Way* were never intended to appear as they do in their published forms. What we got were, at best, roughly outlined notes that make limited technical sense without step-by-step instruction.

Without a technical core from which to draw, people have fixated on the philosophical principles of JKD. But merely spouting philosophy does not make someone a JKD practitioner.

We began our journey with some words from Takuan Soho, so it's only fitting that we should end in the same way:

> There is such a thing as training in principle, and such a thing as training in technique.
>
> Principle is: when you arrive, nothing is noticed. It is simply as though you had discarded all concentration.

If you do not train in technique, but only fill your breast with principle, your body and your hands will not function. Training in technique, if put into terms of our own martial art, is in the training that if practiced over and over again makes the five body postures one.

Even though you know principle, you must make yourself perfectly free in the use of technique. And even though you may wield the sword that you carry with you well, if you are unclear on the deepest aspects of principle, you will likely fall short of proficiency.

Technique and principle are just like the two wheels of a cart.[10]

For several decades now, people have been trying to roll their JKD cart with one wheel. It is beyond the scope of this book to address the philosophical side of JKD, and besides, it is more than adequately accounted for by John Little's excellent cataloguing of Bruce Lee's own words.[11]

What I've given you here is a part of the other wheel, if you will—the technical wheel. This documentation of the hows and whys of the straight lead is an attempt to recover some of what has been lost through misinterpretation, misrepresentation, and the ambition and personal advancement of certain individuals. As Ted Wong told *Black Belt* magazine, "You have to preserve [Bruce Lee's] art at some point to prevent it from completely disappearing. Otherwise, he's just a name; he died and he's gone. So right or wrong, that's my desire—to preserve Bruce Lee's Jeet Kune Do. I'm [sharing my knowledge] to honor him."[12]

And so the purpose of this book—its ultimate aim—has been to honor Bruce Lee.

NOTES

[1] Bruce Lee, ed. John Little, *Jeet Kune Do: Bruce Lee's Commentaries on the Martial Way* (Boston: Tuttle Publishing, 1997), p. 385.

[2] Ibid. p. 50.

[3] John R. Little, *Bruce Lee: A Warrior's Journey* (Chicago: Contemporary Books, 2001), p. 116.

[4] Ibid., p. 115.

[5] Ibid., p. 115.

[6] Ibid., p. 115.

[7] Ibid., p. 117.

[8] Bruce Lee, ed. John Little, *Bruce Lee: Artist of Life* (Boston: Tuttle Publishing, 1999), pp. 165.

[9] Remember from *Enter the Dragon*: "I do not hit. It hits all by itself!"

[10] Takuan Soho, trans. William Scott Wilson (New York: Kodansha International Ltd., 2002), p. 37.

[11] As of this writing, Tuttle has published six volumes of *Bruce Lee Library* series.

[12] Jim Coleman, "Is Bruce Lee's Jeet Kune Do Disappering?" *Black Belt*, July 1990, p. 29.

AN INTERVIEW
WITH TED WONG

Ted Wong is probably the only man, other than Bruce Lee himself, qualified to advise on the how-to's of the most advanced stages of JKD. As Bruce Lee's personal Daytimers reveal, Wong was Bruce Lee's private student from July 27, 1967 to October 14, 1971 and spent more time in private instruction with Bruce than any other individual. The Daytimers show the two had a minimum of 122 separate appointments together.[1, 2] Wong received Jeet Kune Do certification directly from Bruce Lee himself.

As M. Uyehara wrote in *Bruce Lee: The Incomparable Fighter*:

> I still think Bruce considered Ted Wong as his protégé before his death. Wong was his constant companion for the last few years. Besides working out on Wednesday nights, Wong also came to see Bruce on weekends. When Bruce needed a sparring partner, it was Wong he selected.[3]

But records and testimonial aside, one need only observe Ted Wong demonstrate JKD techniques to see that no one else moves more like Bruce. That he is still performing those techniques with more skill, precision, and power than he did over three decades ago is a testament to the fundamental principles of Jeet Kune Do.

Could you explain how Bruce came to look into boxing and fencing literature as influences on JKD?

I don't know exactly when he started to look into Dempsey and Nadi. Back in 1963 he had an altercation with the kung fu artist from China. That was the birth of Jeet Kune Do. He realized that what he had learned was not that functional. A fight that should have taken a few seconds took him three minutes to finish. After that he realized he was not really in shape and started to look for a way to condition himself. And it forced him to think outside the box. I would say that's the birth of Jeet Kune Do. That one incident caused him to look elsewhere and forced him to look into a better way to train. I think he looked into boxing before that, but he really looked into boxing and fencing as a way to educate himself.

Did he mention Driscoll and Dempsey while you were training with him?

I remember he showed me a picture of Jim Driscoll. (See Figure 121.) I didn't even know who Driscoll was, but he looked into Driscoll's books, I would say, around 1968. I was at his home and he mentioned Driscoll. According to boxing historians, he threw the purest, straightest lead hand. He knocked people out with the jab. I think because of the structure, his alignment. When he threw a punch, he really transferred all the weight into it. No boxer has thrown a punch like that. Bruce showed me the picture of Driscoll and said you turn sideways and line up like this to throw the lead punch. You know, no boxing jab is thrown like that now. It's always squared off. Driscoll really gave him the idea of how to throw the lead hand. Wing Chun doesn't throw that way. Boxing doesn't throw that way. So Driscoll gave him the idea of how to utilize the lead hand. And also fencing. I would not say the lead hand came from only Driscoll, or only Dempsey, or only fencing, but the thought—the ideas—came from them. And even in boxing, they do not really tell you the mechanics— the weight distribution, the structure. How you structure your stance determines how you deliver your punch. The structure of Jeet Kune Do, the stance, is more like a fencer's stance. So, when you deliver the front hand, it's more like a sword thrust. All the movement and mobility, the tactics, how to bridge the gap, the speed, how to deliver the lead punch, the strategy all come from fencing.

Did he mention Nadi to you?

No.

How did you know to go to him?

In his library, I noticed *On Fencing* was here. Later on, I traced some of Bruce Lee's notes to it. A lot of the *Tao* is notes that come from boxing and fencing. You can trace the notes—some even word for word from certain books. Like Nadi's book, Dempsey, a lot from Haislet. Later on, when I started to collect boxing books, I knew that he had copies of these books, too. So by reading them and comparing notes, little by little, I realized where things were coming from. There are a lot of things coming from other books, too— not just Haislet.

Figure 120: Bruce Lee and Ted Wong (© Linda Lee Cadwell).

Figure 121: *The picture that Bruce Lee showed Ted Wong to illustrate straight punching. According to Wong, Lee pointed to this photo and said, "You throw the straight lead like this."*

In the Tao, there's a lot of Castello. Is there a lot of Castello in the straight lead?

Yeah, the way he delivered the lead hand. Very few boxers delivered the lead hand like Dempsey. Dempsey would talk about the thumbs up. And the way Driscoll threw the straight is very much like the way [Bruce] would deliver the lead hand.

During the time that he was working with you, did he mention Dempsey?

He mentioned Dempsey, different boxers, the old timers. In fact, sometimes he would ask me if I knew of certain boxers from the '40s through the '60s like Sugar Ray Robinson and Rocky Marciano, Jack Johnson. Even before I took up martial arts, boxing was one of my interests. I didn't practice it, but I read a lot about it. I'd read Marciano's book. I bought every issue of *Ring Magazine.* So, when Bruce would ask me if I knew of certain boxers, I would know, so he was kind of surprised. That's why he opened up to me when discussing boxing.

Did he discuss specific things from Dempsey that he was incorporating?

See Bruce Lee pretty much kept a lot of things to himself. Even in a letter he wrote to William Cheung, he said not to share with anybody—keep it to yourself. Occasionally he'd tell me something, but what I learned from him—half was through instruction. The other half was through observation. Maybe I'm one of the lucky few who was able to spend a lot of time with him training. A lot of times, he used me as a sparring partner. So, I could watch his moves. The way he'd move. The timing, the footwork. So, I learned a lot from him through observation. If I didn't have that kind of time with him, I'd never, never have learned from him.

So, in terms of mechanics, what kind of things did he actually show you?

The rotational movement, the alignment, how to transfer the weight thumbs up. How to put the hip into it. The structure of the stance. He explained only a little bit. Later on, I started collecting the books myself and then I would see that all of those things were coming from certain books. Even things like the hand before foot was not being taught at the school. That was something he showed us at his home. Most of the time it was just him and me, or Herb Jackson [another student of Bruce Lee's who also built much of Lee's custom training equip- ment] and me at his home. Every Wednesday. Sometimes Sunday with a group. But with a group it was just basically a workout. I think at that time he was still sort of experimenting.

So, you got to see a lot of that experimentation?

Yeah. But at that time, he wouldn't always fully explain what he was working on. He might just say turn the hip into it, thumbs up, hand before foot, but he wouldn't go into a lot of detail.

And you also have photocopies of his books with his notes in them?

Oh yeah. See, nobody has those notes. You can buy the books, but Bruce Lee had written notes in his copies, underlined things.

What did he show you in terms of footwork?

Half the footwork he just showed me how to perform. The other half I learned by looking at him. The way he moved and transferred the weight. And then I was able to put them together later on, a little bit at a time. Most of this stuff I discovered. All of the little details I learned later on. The movement, the understanding through observation. The really intricate movement, gaining insight into each movement, and the reason behind each one—I basically discovered through years of practice, over and over again. And then a little bit at a time, I started to understand why.

Like the stealing step?

Yeah, a lot of things I didn't understand and I could not do, I could not even perform, at the beginning. But now I can. It's still the original footwork. I'm not adding things to it. I can show you a certain punch. But without footwork, you can only do it a certain way. You're one-dimensional. Footwork makes you three-dimensional, giving you more options. With footwork, you can throw the same punch but in any direction. Without footwork, you can only throw a punch one way. With footwork, you can throw clockwise, counterclockwise, while moving forward, moving backward.

Did the footwork he showed you at the school differ from what he showed you in the backyard?

The footwork in the Chinatown school was more like one-beat footwork. There's no bounce, no half-beat, very little curving. We called it step-through curving or pivoting. The footwork he taught me at his house was much more in depth as far as application. He talked about the bounce, the half-beat. Those things make footwork more alive.

Were you the only person he showed that to?

Herb was there, too. Other than that, I don't know.

Did you see a progression in the development of the straight lead while you were studying with him?

Oh yeah. At the beginning, I saw that when he'd throw a lead hand, there was a little curving or arcing, especially on retracting the hand. Later on, it was much more straight, straight in and straight out—much more compact and more protection of the center line. So nowadays, I still see people throwing with the curving arc, showing that they learned the lead punch from him earlier on.

What do you think are the best examples of the straight on film because there was a lot of development of that punch between the time of The Big Boss *and* Game of Death.

I do have the footage of the backyard training session, but he doesn't really throw many there. Just the straight blast. Last year at the Bruce Lee convention in Burbank there was some incredible footage of Bruce sparring throwing straight lead after straight.[4]

If you were to look at all the movies, probably the best example with the most JKD in it is *Return of the Dragon* with Chuck Norris. I think that movie has more JKD in it than any of his other films. He does a lot of intercepting kicking and punching. Of course, it's set up to be theatrical, but you can see a lot of JKD in there.

In that final fight scene, there's a sequence that's slowed down. He keeps his hand pretty low. Is that how he looked when he sparred?

Basically when you sparred him, he wasn't moving like in the movies where he was bouncing around. He wouldn't move that much. He'd stay in front of you, not moving at all. Sometimes he'd move a little bit. But when he'd attack, he was so quick. That sudden motion from stillness would make it more difficult for you to detect or guard against his motion. But when he had to move, he could move! That's the way he'd fight. Not like in the movies. So, all that footwork, you don't use it until the situation calls for it. You don't bounce unnecessarily. He'd move and then stop, change the tempo. He was always doing something to change it up a little, but not like the movies where he would be moving, moving, moving.

In *Enter the Dragon*, there's a lot of wide motion. A lot of swinging. The scene with Bob Wall is a very good example of how to hit without telegraphing. We did that a lot at his home just like a game. It's a good example of the push-off. You really have to come in, because when your hand is crossed with your opponent, you're standing further away from each other. So if you were to extend your hand, you're not going to reach him. So, you have to push off to go beyond the target. The hand has to move first and come back without your opponent touching you. The hand has to move first. The same is true of trapping. See, a lot of people trap first and then hit. They think trapping is primary, and hitting is secondary. In Jeet Kune Do, hitting is primary. Trapping is secondary. So, trapping is just basically to remove the barrier.

Did he talk about Newton with you?

Oh yeah, action and reaction. The same way we do. He'd line you up and then tap your fist.

Oh, did he do that same test that you do?[5]

Not at the school. But at his home, when he first started to teach me, he'd have me put my fist on the wall like in the Dempsey book. Or when we'd do push-ups. He'd have us try it with the bottom three knuckles or the top three knuckles. And then we'd change the way we'd line up. This wasn't being taught at the class, but at private lessons.

Did he talk at all about ways to strategically incorporate the straight lead?

He talked about how when you throw a straight lead, you cover the centerline. He also said it's quicker to recover from. He said a good punch deviates as little as from the on-guard as possible. You should also return to on-guard as quickly as possible. Any punch that meets that criteria is a good punch. Anytime you deviate from the stance, you open up the center. He also pointed out that the straight can be used for offense and defense. You can use it to keep your opponent at bay. It's the quickest punch and also enables you to apply force, not like a boxing jab. This allows you to set things up. Or you can use it as a single direct attack, because the straight lead is a power punch. Once you have a good single direct attack, the rest is easy if you're going to use PIA. The straight is very important to set up the other ways of attack. If you don't have that, the rest will be kind of difficult for you. On Jeet Kune Do, the strategy is built around the lead hand.

Did he discuss how the straight can be used for setups?

When we were sparring he did explain that. And also when I was sparring with him, I'd see what he did to me, so I'd understand how to use the lead hand. But most of the time, he didn't explain to me in detail. All those small details I discovered later on. Driscoll talked about the four hits—hit first, hit hard, hit often, hit straight. For setup's the front hand is so important. It's the quickest. The way we throw it, you have power. It may not be the most powerful punch, but it's more powerful than a boxing jab. The boxing jab doesn't compare in terms of power. You also have extra reach with the JKD lead. What makes the JKD punch so effective is that the way we stand is pretty much lined up with the target. You give away very little. And when you make a move, you move very little—only to cover distance. When you move, the rotation's so quick. That combined with the footwork enables you to reach the target quicker than any other punch. So, the lead hand plus the footwork makes the straight the fastest punch. The backfist is a little faster, but there's a little less power, and you feel more of the impact because you're hitting with the back of your hand.

How does your technique now compare to the way it was when you were studying with Bruce?

It took me six months to get the feel of it. And then it took me all these years to refine it. At the beginning, I still had to think. Now I don't think when I hit. Now I understand what he meant by, "I do not hit. It hits all by itself." It takes years to understand the technique, all the small details, and how to use it. You can throw all sorts of punches against pieces of paper, mitts, and bags. It won't do you any good unless you can judge the distance with a moving target. That skill only comes with actual application. That's why Bruce always emphasized sparring. That's how he honed the technique. At the beginning, the feeling comes from two things. The first is the mechanics and the sequence of motion. You can feel every body part moving, every joint. That takes a long time to learn. The three-point landing, you have to feel. The fist has to land first, the front leg, then the back leg. Then you can't really understand that until you can apply it by sparring. When you start to spar, that's a whole new ballgame. Bruce said that being able to hit an opponent with a good combination is satisfying, but if you can hit the target with one shot, then that's a sign of greatness. The front hand lead gives you that. You need timing, distance, to be nontelegraphic, footwork.

Can you talk a little more about the position of the front hand and the variations?

To be fast, you want to use the gunsight. If you watch Bruce Lee's hand, it's like this here [demonstrates]. If your hand is pointed down, then your hand has to come up before you can aim at the target. So, if you really want to hit somebody quickly, you want to use the gunsight. But then again, you need to learn how to hit with your hand up or down. In JKD, we have three ranges—long, middle, and close. Long range is like kicking distance. The middle range is where you throw the lead and use combinations. At close range, you can use trapping and bent-arm punching. At long range, you keep the hand down. You move better with that hand down, and you can see your opponent better. Also, Bruce used to say if his hand was down he could hook, uppercut, throw low or high. That's why he preferred it that way. It's also less threatening, so it's like attack by drawing. But you have to first learn how to throw a straight lead with the hand up, from what I'd call the standard stance. But once you have mobility, footwork, and upper body evasion, you don't have to keep the hand up. The better boxers do that. Boxers that have good upper body movement and footwork don't keep their front hand up. Keeping that front hand down gives you better balance. It keeps that extra weight lower.

What are the differences between boxing and JKD?

What makes JKD different from boxing is the range. In boxing the range is I can touch you, and you can touch me. In JKD, it's a half-step back. I can touch you, but you cannot touch me. When we attack, though, we have to cover ground with the push-off to reach you. But if you don't train that way, you just step in to cover distance. Also the front hand lead is more like a single straight thrust. It's the most difficult attack in fencing. And the straight lead is the most difficult attack in JKD. It's a very unnatural thing to do, because the hand moves before the feet. When you walk, the hands and feet move at the same time. With the straight lead, you also have to cover greater distance, so you have to have the footwork, the push-off.

Why don't we see boxers straight punching today?

Good question. Boxing's more like entertainment now. People would get bored watching someone hit and not get hit. They want to see blood, knockouts, toe to toe. It's become a style. They got used to training the way they do. Today boxers are physically stronger and faster. Their conditioning makes up for not having the advantages of a straight lead. Some boxers, like Ali and De La Hoya, do have a good jab, but they are not punching like the old timers—not like Bruce, with the thumbs up. You cannot apply the thumbs up structure with today's boxing stance, which is more swing-oriented. The straight lead is a long-range punch. The straight lead has become something of a lost art. It takes a long time to cultivate. People get frustrated. They don't understand the principle or the structure behind it. Straight hitting has become a forgotten art. If Bruce Lee were alive today, I think he'd agree that boxing really hasn't improved. In fact, it's regressed. Dempsey and Driscoll were saying that in the '20s.

What is it that makes the straight so difficult? Would you say it's the most difficult technique in JKD?

Yes. Look at Nadi's book. He says the single, straight thrust is the most difficult technique in fencing. So the typical front hand lead in JKD is, according to Bruce Lee, the most diffi-cult technique in JKD. The fencing single, straight thrust and the Jeet Kune Do straight lead parallel each other. It's easy to throw a bent-arm punch and swing. When men first start to punch, it's not a straight punch. Throwing a straight punch is difficult and requires more sci-ence to it. When I was a little kid, and I wanted to fight, the first thing I did was just to swing. The straight punch came late in fistic history. It required more science. That's why Bruce Lee liked it. That's why it's difficult. If it was easy, everybody would be using it. The Jeet Kune Do straight punch is an educated punch. It takes understanding of body alignment, leverage. Swinging is easy. Everybody can throw a swing. But to throw a straight punch takes education and understanding.

Did Bruce ever talk about the difficulty of straight punching?

Oh yeah, because most schools cannot comprehend the principles of that punch. Most peo-ple cannot get a good feeling throwing it. So when I started teaching it, people would give up. Some people said, "Oh, it won't work." They think they can't get power from it. It takes a lot of practice. As you start to do it correctly, little by little, you'll start to get power.

N O T E S

[1] Ted Wong with John Little, *Bruce Lee's Lead Punch: Ted Wong Explains Jun Fan Jeet Kine Do's Most Explosive Technique!* June, 2000, pp. 58. According to John Little the actual number of meetings between Bruce Lee and Ted Wong may be much higher than 122.

[2] Bruce Lee, ed. John Little, *Jeet Kune Do: Bruce Lee's Commentaries on the Martial Way* (Boston: Tuttle Publishing, 1997), p. 14.

[3] M. Uyehara, *Bruce Lee: The Incomparable Fighter* (Santa Clarita, CA: Ohara Publications, Inc., 1988), pp. 53–55.

[4] At the time of this writing, the footage mentioned here was not yet made available to the public and had only been shown at the Burbank convention.

[5] See the end of the stance chapter in this book.

B I B L I O G R A P H Y

Carpenter, Harry. *Boxing: An Illustrated History*. New York: Crescent Books, 1982.

Castello, Julio Martinez. *The Theory and Practice of Fencing*. New York: Charles Scribner's Sons, 1933.

Cheung, William and Ted Wong. *Wing Chun Kung Fu/Jeet Kune Do: A Comparison, Volume 1*. Santa Clarita, CA: Ohara Publications, Inc., 1990.

Clark, Michael A. and Rodney J. Corn. *NASM Optimum Performance Training for the Fitness Professional*. Calabasas: National Academy of Sports Medicine, 2001.

Cohen, Richard. *By the Sword: A History of Gladiators, Musketeers, Samurai, Swashbucklers, and Olympic Champions*. New York: Random House, 2002.

Dempsey, Jack. *Championship Fighting: Explosive Punching and Aggressive Defence*. New York: Prentice Hall, Inc., 1950.

Driscoll, Jim. *The Straight Left and How to Cultivate It*. London: Athletic Publications, Ltd.

————. *Outfighting or Long Ranging Boxing*. London: Athletic Publications, Ltd.

Frith, Simon. *Performing Rites: On the Value of Popular Music*. Cambridge, MA: Harvard University Press, 1996.

Godfrey, Captain John and W. C. Heinz, ed. "The Useful Science of Defence" in *The Fireside Book of Boxing*. New York: Simon and Schuster, 1961.

Grombach, John V. *The Saga of the Fist*. New York: A.S. Barnes and Company, 1977.

Haislet, Edwin L. *Boxing*. New York: A.S. Barnes & Noble Company, 1940.

Hewitt, Paul G. *Conceptual Physics, 9th Edition*. San Francisco: Addison Wesley, 2002.

Kahn, Roger. *A Flame of Pure Fire: Jack Dempsey and the Roaring '20s*. New York: Harcourt Brace, 1999.

BIBLIOGRAPHY

Lee, Bruce. *Tao of Jeet Kune Do*. Santa Clarita, CA, Ohara Publications, Inc., 1975.

Lee, Bruce and John Little, ed. *Bruce Lee: Artist of Life*. Boston: Tuttle Publishing, 1999.

——. *Jeet Kune Do: Bruce Lee's Commentaries on the Martial Way*. Boston: Tuttle Publishing.

——. *Letters of the Dragon: Correspondence, 1958–1973*. Boston: Tuttle Publishing, 1998.

——. *The Tao of Gung Fu*. Boston: Tuttle Publishing, 1997.

Lee, Bruce and M. Uyehara. *Bruce Lee's Fighting Method*. Burbank, CA: Ohara Publications, Inc.

Little, John R. *Bruce Lee: A Warrior's Journey*. Chicago: Contemporary Books, 2001.

Loehr, James E. *The New Toughness Training for Sports*. New York: Penguin Books, 1995.

Montana, Joe with Richard Weiner. *Joe Montana's Art and Magic of Quarterbacking*. New York: Henry Holt and Company, 1997.

Nadi, Aldo. *On Fencing*. Bangor, ME: Laureate Press, 1994.

Nadi, Aldo and Lance Lobo, ed. *The Living Sword: A Fencer's Autobiography*. Sunrise, FL: Laureate Press, 1995.

Nishioka, Hayward. "Power in the Punch," *The Best of Bruce Lee*. 1974, pp. 72–74.

Prashad, Vijay. "Summer of Bruce" in *Screaming Monkeys*. Minneapolis, MN: Coffee House Press, 2003.

Soho, Takuan and William Scott Wilson, trans. *The Unfettered Mind*. New York: Kodansha International Ltd., 2002.

Uyehara, M. *Bruce Lee: The Incomparable Fighter*. Santa Clarity, CA: Ohara Publications, Inc., 1988.

Wooden, John with Steve Jamison. *Wooden: A Lifetime of Observations and Reflections on and off the Court*. Chicago: Contemporary Books, 1997.

Teri Tom, MS, RD, is a board member of the Bruce Lee Foundation and a certified Jun Fan Jeet Kune Do instructor under Ted Wong and, as of this writing, has spent over 1000 hours in private study with Sifu Wong. Teri is also a registered dietitian with a BA in communications studies from UCLA, a master's degree in nutritional science from California State University, Los Angeles, and a certificate in personal training from the National Academy of Sports Medicine. She specializes in sports nutrition and runs her practice out of the exclusive SportsClub/LA in West Los Angeles.

"Using no way as way; having no limitation as limitation"

THE BRUCE LEE FOUNDATION

The Bruce Lee Foundation, is a California nonprofit 501(c)(3), founded in April of 2002 by Bruce Lee's wife, Linda Lee Cadwell and daughter, Shannon Lee Keasler. The Foundation was created **to preserve and perpetuate the art, philosophy and legacy of Bruce Lee for generations to come**.

The **chief aim** of the Foundation is to serve as a resource for those seeking authentic information about Bruce Lee and his art of Jun Fan Jeet Kune Do®. We endeavor to work at this goal by proactively delivering Bruce Lee's philosophical message, martial way, and life example to the public through a number of venues.

BRUCE LEE FOUNDATION PROGRAMS AND GOALS:

Seminars in Jun Fan Jeet Kune Do
The Bruce Lee Scholarship Program
The Official Bruce Lee Museum
Bruce Lee Conventions and Events
And much, much more . . .

To find out more about Bruce Lee and Jun Fan Jeet Kune Do® visit us at:

www.bruceleefoundation.com.

If you would like to make a donation, add your name to our mailing list, or apply for a scholarship, check the Web site and contact us at:

Bruce Lee Foundation
11693 San Vicente Blvd
Suite 918
Los Angeles, CA 90049

®

Please make checks payable to Bruce Lee Foundation. Your gift is tax deductible to the extent provided by law. Your gift will go to support the Bruce Lee Foundation's current operating budget. For further information, or if you wish to make a gift restricted to a specific purpose (only gifts of $2500.00 or more), please write or send your specified gift to Bruce Lee Foundation, 11693 San Vicente Blvd, Suite 918, Los Angeles, CA 90049. Thank you for your support!